RACISM@WORK AMONG THE LORD'S PEOPLE

Questions That We All Need to Ask Ourselves about Prejudice, Bigotry and Racism During the 21st Century

ROBERT UPTON

FOREWORDS BY DR. ED DOBSON AND SCOTT HAGAN

insight
PUBLISHING GROUP

Tulsa, Oklahoma

RACISM@WORK AMONG THE LORD'S PEOPLE

Racism@Work Among the LORD'*s People* by Robert Upton

Published by Insight Publishing Group
8801 S. Yale, Suite 410
Tulsa, OK 74137
918-493-1718

Unless otherwise noted all Scripture quotations are taken from the New International Version of the Bible. Copyright © 1973, 1978, 1984 by International Bible Society. Used by permission of Zondervan Publishing House. Scripture quotations marked NAS are taken from the New American Standard Bible. Copyright © 1960, 1962, 1963, 1968, 1971, 1972, 1973, 1975, 1977, 1995 by the Lockman Foundation. Used by permission.

ISBN 1-930027-89-3

Library of Congress catalog card number: 2003104263

Printed in the United States of America

Robert Upton has put together a marvelous new book that will not only *deliver* you, but will also give you the vocabulary to become a *deliverer* of people. The human soul can detect instantly whether or not it is being celebrated or tolerated. Robert Upton's book will help that truth come alive in your heart.

-Scott Hagan, Senior Pastor and author, Grand Rapids First Assembly of God Church, Grand Rapids, Michigan

As one called to be a "bridge builder" in the Body of Christ, it is refreshing to see a book that engages the reader and calls us to examine our roles in perpetuating the evil of racial prejudice and racism. *Racism@Work Among the LORD'S People* allows everyone to take a step towards being a part of the solution, rather than a part of the problem.

-Babbie Mason, Christian Recording Artist, songwriter and author

There is nothing as powerful as a question. Questions demand an exposure of our hearts. The Scriptures teach that out of the heart the mouth speaks. The implication is that our speech reveals our deepest convictions. In this work, Robert Upton's unique approach to this sensitive issue brings a fresh perspective for all of us. I encourage you to read and honestly assess your answers to these critical questions. These questions can bring healing and answers to your life. The question is, can you answer these questions?

-Dr. Myles E. Munroe, President, Senior Pastor and author, Bahamas Faith Ministries International, Nassau, Bahamas

This book is a must-read! The church needs to embrace racial and cultural diversity, and begin to reach out to those who have been hurt or wounded because of prejudice, bigotry, and racism. I believe that this book is a great resource for those who desire to do more in the area of racial reconciliation.

-Mario Murillo, Evangelist and author, San Ramon, California

I pray that this book can be another piece that could lead us closer to the area of reconciliation or to that oneness that Jesus prayed for when He asked that we might be one, so that the world would know we were Christians because of our love for one another.

- Dr. John M. Perkins, President and author, John M. Perkins Foundation for Reconciliation & Development, Jackson, Mississippi

Robert Upton has combined the Socratic method of asking questions and the challenge of examining our own hearts to give us wise counsel on how to overcome the destructive issues of bigotry, prejudice, and racism. His wisdom gained through personal experience and Godly training will help the Church move from talking about these issues to acting on these issues. The Church can only ignore Upton's challenges at her own peril.

-John Raymond, Associate Publisher, Zondervan Publishing House, Grand Rapids, Michigan

This book surfaces a gold mine of questions that all Christians should be asking themselves about racism, prejudice, and bigotry. Honest responses to those questions will inevitably disturb the realities of many people—hopefully leading them to take positive steps toward Christ-inspired social justice. On issues of race and equality, Christians should be taking the lead toward the finish line of equality. Reading this book may help us get out of the starting blocks.

-Dr. Steve L. Robbins, Director, Woodrick Institute for the Study of Racism and Diversity, Grand Rapids, Michigan

Robert has a basic and good understanding of racial issues. With these questions, willing people of all races are confronted into dealing with the racism that they may have hidden in their hearts.

-Dr. Duane G. Vander Klok, Senior Pastor and author, Resurrection Life Church, Grandville, Michigan

In just a few years, America will be the most racially diverse nation in all human history. The challenge to establish cross-racial relationships is increasing while the success rate continues to decrease. We need new models and experiences or otherwise we will face a national relational disaster. This book will help us to avoid the latter.

-Dr. Raleigh B. Washington, Executive Vice-President of Global Ministries and author, Promise Keepers, Denver, Colorado

THIS BOOK IS WRITTEN IN MEMORY OF:

Evangelist Harry Dunn
October 8, 1934 - March 28, 2001

Harry Dunn was the former Pastor of the Evangelistic Center, which is based in Grand Rapids, Michigan. I don't personally know anyone that loved poor and hurting people more than the late evangelist Harry Dunn. He totally abandoned pursuing wealth, pleasure, riches, and fame so he could clothe the naked and feed the poor. Harry took everything he had and made a significant investment into the lives of many people that had been discarded by society.

Harry was a man who had an extremely close relationship with God. When a doctor once told Harry that his son would be born dead in the womb, he prayed and God told him that his baby was alive! Harry believed God enough to tell the doctor that his baby was alive! The doctor went into the delivery room and came running down the hallway proclaiming that Harry's baby boy was alive and what happened was a miracle.

Rev. Donnell Smith
June 29, 1956 - November 1, 1998

Rev. Donnell Smith labored as pastor of New Hope Missionary Baptist Church, which is located in Grand Rapids, Michigan, for more than ten years. Reverend Smith was never afraid to address the issues of racial injustice and inequality from the pulpit. He was a husband, father, brother, preacher, teacher, leader, friend, and advocate for the poor and downcast. Most notable among Reverend Smith's accomplishments were leading a successful effort to build elderly housing, launching a capital campaign drive to build a multipurpose center for youth, convincing the National Baptist Convention of America to host their annual convention in Grand Rapids, Michigan, and threatening to sue the Grand Rapids Board of Education if they refused to hire the first African-American female superintendent, who happened to be the most qualified candidate to lead the school district at the time.

Rev. Smith's memory lives on today through his two daughters, Danielle, Gabrielle and their mother Michelle Smith-Lowe. It is through his life that I have come to understand that the Christian life is filled with tears of joy and sorrow, success and failure, and obedience and disobedience. But more importantly, it is filled with God's grace, forgiveness, and unconditional love.

CONTENTS

DEDICATION

This book is dedicated to the following persons:

To my wife: I would like to thank you for your support and your prayers for this project. You are definitely a beautiful gift from God! You are a wonderful helpmate and my best friend. Thanks for being a wonderful mother to our children, Alexis and Devin. I would like to thank you for reviewing the manuscript and providing me with helpful suggestions and feedback, which have served to greatly enhance the quality of the book.

To my daughter: Daddy loves you very much! Your mom and I could never have imagined how much joy you would bring to us when we brought you home from the hospital. You are a special gift from God. I love it when you yell, "Daddy!" and run and jump into my arms. What a beautiful picture of reality this has been for me! You have very consistently reminded me of how much God desires for me to have the heart of a child when it comes to running and jumping into His loving arms and enjoying the life-changing experience.

To my son: You are an awesome gift from God! I look forward to seeing you grow up and seeing you realize your full potential in God. It is my fervent prayer that you will be able to do great things for the Kingdom of God! You have added even more joy, excitement, and happiness to our family. Daddy loves you very much!

To my parents: Thanks for planting seeds about Jesus Christ into my life at an early age. This has played a major role in helping me to discover what God's plan was for my life. I do not believe that I would have discovered that God had a call on my life for ministry if neither one of you would have taken time to deposit life-changing spiritual seeds into my heart. May God give me the wisdom to plant the same type of spiritual seeds into my children's hearts that will produce good fruit much like the seeds that both of you deposited into my life.

FOREWORD

Racism is alive and well in the United States. It is not as blatant as it used to be. It's not as obvious as it used to be. It's not as public as it used to be. But it nonetheless is! Laws may prevent discrimination in the public square, but no law can change a person's heart.

Unfortunately, in the long struggle to overcome racism and bigotry, the Church has been as much a part of the problem as it has been part of the solution. The A.M.E. church and many other African-American denominations exist as a result of flawed white theology and practice. These churches were established because black people were not accepted as equal within the white churches. This divide, which goes all the way back to slavery, continues to exist today. Black and white churches are only miles apart geographically, but are hundreds of miles apart spiritually.

Talking about race is most difficult for us in the white community. We are afraid of saying the wrong thing, so we tend to be polite and seldom get to the real issues that divide us. But the time has come for honest, biblically-rooted discussion. Robert Upton provides us with a book that will help us talk and ultimately change. This is the most remarkable book I have ever seen dealing with racism and bigotry because it is filled with questions. There are questions that we all must faceblack and white together. Many of them are profoundly uncomfortable. This is a book rooted in the ancient Rabbinical teaching method—keep asking questions. The time has come for us to begin addressing these questions and answering them before God.

-Dr. Ed Dobson, Senior Pastor, Calvary Church, Grand Rapids, Michigan

FOREWORD

Wandering in the dark through a dangerous construction zone is neither the wisest nor safest thing to do. But don't tell that to Nehemiah. Driven by faith to know the facts, Nehemiah embarked on a midnight reconnaissance mission to scrutinize the reconstruction progress of the Jerusalem wall. But what he found was more of the same—rubble. The reports had proven true.

Good men with great ambitions had sojourned before him with dreams of doing something historic for God. Ninety-four years before Nehemiah, it was Zerubbabel whom God first tagged to lead the delegation of captives back to Jerusalem. His intent was to rebuild the ruins of a now post-exilic Israel. Following Zerubbabel, it was Ezra who sought to rekindle the rebuilding efforts. Both of these godly men, however, were unable to fully accomplish the dreams God had placed in their hearts.

It was that very incompleteness that gnawed most at Nehemiah and haunted his belief system. Regardless of what lay beneath his feet that night as he surveyed the wall, Nehemiah still believed God had the savvy to restore the Holy City, though ninety-four years of rubble said it was impossible.

Trading in his cupbearing comforts for a shovel and sword, Nehemiah cried out to God and cracked the code. Suddenly God achieved through His people in fifty-two days what they had not allowed Him to achieve in over nine decades.

For the past nine decades, the church in America has similarly been beset by horrible incompletes. But does anyone really care? Yes, good people have been active, but can we honestly say we are where God wants us as a nation when it comes to racial unity?

At the turn of the twentieth Century, we experienced our most historic and revered revival, Azusa Street—a revival that we somehow have romanticized while losing sight of what made it so potentially special to God's Kingdom. For nearly three years, Azusa Street bloodied the lip of racial prejudice and hatred that saturated a post-slavery America. God was healing our land.

For a brief period in time, the two races chose to race together. But as with Zerubbabel and Ezra, the work was never completed. The power of social conditioning put a chokehold on the newly revitalized Church, and the real miracle of Azusa was abandoned.

Interestingly, Azusa Street as a historical revival event is claimed by both predominantly black and white denominations as their own. Yet as it was for Nehemiah, almost no discernable change has occurred in the ninety-six years since Azusa Street. Our cities remain socially and spiritually bankrupt while denominations lob their lifeless messages of reconciliation from behind their cultural walls. Yes, we do well with the easy stuff like smiling, shaking hands, and respectfully patting one another on the shoulder, but when the day is done, our hearts remain fearfully disengaged.

It is now 2003, and unless a new generation of Nehemiahs are discovered and a new innovation within the church is released, our legacy of unity will be nothing more than the rearranged rubble of hesitancy and indifference, where proclamations and symbolism prevail over real substance and functional togetherness.

Destiny begins with dignity. Jesus was the master at depositing dignity into people. One simple way white America can demonstrate the dignity of Christ is by showing compassion for the plight of black America outside the Church and not just inside the Church. At times, the sensitivities of white America seem imprisoned by the limited view of our own dealings with black Christians in the lobby of our local churches. And because we cannot identify any personal actions we deem racist on our part, we quietly convince ourselves that black America for the most part is whining or overdoing it when it comes to racial issues.

Let's be honest: most white Christians give no thought to the educational and economic injustices that touch many black and brown believers in America. Our only paradigm is through Church eyes and ultra-brief hellos in church hallways, all of which insulate us from the real life roadblocks that many of our black friends face in the marketplace.

Yes, there are many friendly churches in America, but what we lack is the desire, vocabulary, and mechanisms for aggressively healing the collateral pain of many Americans who have been oppressed by the theological and secular injustices that surround them twenty-four hours a day. The genuine love of Jesus flowing through His Church is what helps pay off the debt of pain this nation has caused to so many people. And the Cross of Christ is the master key. Jesus was the archetype of unconditional inclusion. He wanted people healed, and He wanted them with Him in relationship. Jesus wasn't about healing people and sending them on their way. He was about healing them so they could follow Him in relationship.

Robert Upton is doing all of that and more. I know Robert. He and his beautiful wife worship God faithfully in the church I pastor, as well as model every principle laid forth in this book. You can trust him. But more than trust him, I hope you will join him and become an active part of America's new healing army.

-Scott Hagan, Senior Pastor, Grand Rapids First Assembly of God, Grand Rapids, Michigan

PREFACE

Racism@Work Among the LORD'S People is a book that poses powerful and thought-provoking questions to the reader about prejudice, bigotry, and racism. The book is not designed to answer questions. Instead, the reader must work through each question for himself. God will reveal whether or not the reader harbors any prejudice, bigotry, or racism in his heart. Rodney King, shortly after the Los Angeles riots, in a hastily called press conference asked a very profound question as he appealed for calm. Mr. King asked the following question, "Can we all just get along?" How you respond to the questions in this book will ultimately determine whether or not the answer to the question is yes or no.

Racism is definitely a spiritual issue. No one can seriously begin to address the issues of bigotry, prejudice, and racism until she has first done a self-examination of her own heart. If she fails to make a genuine effort to deal with her own heart, then it is highly unlikely that her words will ever translate to any action that could possibly lead to meaningful change. Therefore, neither the individual nor the organization she leads will become successful change agents that will cause the environment around them to change. Without individuals or the organizations they represent actively taking the necessary steps to address bigotry, prejudice, and racism, these very evil and destructive forces will continue to spread like a spiritual cancer.

No person or institution has been immune from the temptation to be prejudiced, bigoted, or racist. While the world has grappled quite a lot with these very explosive and volatile spiritual issues, for a good portion of Church history, neither Christians as individuals or the Church as an institution has done much to address or eradicate these problems. Therefore, as a result, we are now as a nation reaping the results of our own sin.

Most churches are still segregated on Sunday morning in America. Many churches that are predominantly white across America are dying because they do not feel comfortable, do not understand, or simply do not want to reach out to neighborhoods located right in their backyards because they have become considerably racially diverse. God is in the process of birthing many new wineskins for Church ministry that celebrate diversity and are racially inclusive, while many of the old wine-skins for Church ministry that do not really value diversity and are racially exclusive are in the process of dying a slow but quiet death.

Churches that refuse to change their outreach efforts to effectively reach out to people from diverse racial and cultural backgrounds will either be forced to rediscover their church mission, move, or cease to exist. A large number of these churches will have for sale signs in front of their church buildings and property in the near future. Many of these churches will be replaced by congregations that primarily consist of persons of color from the same racial background or by multiethnic congregations. The postmodern world that has ushered in so much change and uncertainty is now forcing many churches to change so they can become more effective in reaching out to a world where the Church as an institution seems to have lost much of its influence.

With the racial landscape around churches across America changing at a very rapid pace, the pressure will continue to increase upon the Church as an institution to change in order to remain relevant in a world that is constantly changing. This change will impact urban churches, suburban churches, and rural churches.

Many urban churches are now located in neighborhoods where the racial makeup has drastically changed. As a result, urban churches that primarily consist of people from the same race will need to begin reaching out to persons from other racial and cultural backgrounds. Some of these churches will eventually be forced to reexamine their outreach efforts as new multiethnic church models are introduced within their communities. Given the projected changes in the racial composition of the U.S. population, churches of non-color located within suburban communities will have to begin to take the subject of diversity seriously. These churches will have to begin to reach out to persons of color or many of these churches will not survive as the U.S. population becomes more racially diverse. We can expect to see more multi-ethnic church models for ministry emerging as the population becomes even more racially diverse. While the percentage of multi-ethnic churches in the United States only represents three percent of churches, this number is expected to greatly increase in the future.[1] Rural churches will continue to be impacted by urban sprawl and the arrival of other churches within their communities.

Racism@Work Among the LORD'S People provides pastors and laypersons with some helpful suggestions that will encourage them to foster greater racial unity in the Body of Christ. A comprehensive analysis of demographic trends for the U.S. population has been provided, and more importantly, the direct implications that these trends will have on the Church as in an institution are thoroughly examined. The Appendixes Section includes a Resource list of consultants, organizations, and government agencies where further information or assistance can be obtained. Ten Best Practices have been provided to assist the reader in developing cross-cultural friendships/relationships and racially diverse organizations. Also, a Definition of Terms page has been included that will provide the reader with practical definitions for the terms prejudice, bigotry, and racism. The reader will be able to review Prejudice, Bigoted and Racist Thoughts/Statements that can impede progress in achieving racial diversity within the church. A Suggested Reading Section has been included that provides the reader with a list of other books that have been published on the topic of racism. A Self-Assessment Tool has also been included that will enable the reader to set goals and identify practical action steps that can be taken to help foster racial unity.

ACKNOWLEDGMENTS

I would like to begin by thanking John Mason, the owner of Insight Publishing Group (IPG) for his wisdom, insight, and genuine interest in the subject matter of this book. The IPG staff should be commended for their commitment to excellence and for the many hours they have invested to ensure that this project is an absolute success!

Many thanks to the following persons that have either reviewed the manuscript, issued endorsement statements, or made other contributions that have greatly enhanced the quality of the finished product: Marilyn Burnett Abplanalp, Che Ahn, Reverend Joseph Barndt, Dr. Samuel R. Chand, Dr. Susan E. Davies, Dick DeVos, Jr., Dr. Ed Dobson, Connie Edwards, Dr. Michael O. Emerson, Dr. Joe R. Feagin, Bishop Joseph L. Garlington, Sr., Michael E. Goings, Reverend Billy Graham, Dr. David Ireland, Bishop T.D. Jakes, Greg Laurie, Josh Lease (Editor), Dr. John Lee, Suzette Long, Babbie Mason, Brian D. McLaren, Coach Bill McCartney, Reverend Patricia Mills, Mario Murillo, Dr. Myles E. Monroe, Clarence Page, Dr. John M. Perkins, Rachelle Hood-Phillips, John Raymond, Chris Rice, Dr. Steve L. Robbins, Dr. Duane G. Vander Klok , Dr. George Yancey, Dr. Raleigh B. Washington, Jim Wallis and Bob Woodrick.

I would like to personally thank Pastor Scott and Karen Hagan for their friendship, love, and support. They have been called to pastor one of the best churches in America! Grand Rapids First Assembly of God Church has become a great place of healing where people from diverse racial, cultural, socioeconomic backgrounds can come together and celebrate the diversity of the cross. Also, I would to acknowledge and personally thank Julian and Tiffany Newman who serve on the pastoral team at Grand Rapids First Assembly of God for their friendship, love, and prayers.

No words could ever convey my love and appreciation for all of the people that have helped me gain a greater insight and understanding into God's Word and His ways. Although their names will not appear below, their contributions to my life, whether big or small, have not been forgotten nor overlooked.

Finally, I would like to thank all of the persons that are a part of my Daily Bible Scripture e-mail list for providing me with the opportunity to sow God's Word into their lives on a daily basis. This daily journey through the Scriptures has provided me with a wonderful opportunity to develop a more intimate relationship with God.

INTRODUCTION

I am deeply concerned about the failure of the nation's churches to address the issues of prejudice, bigotry, and racism. The results have been disastrous. It seems that a great deal of the efforts that have been made to address these spiritual issues have come from the secular world. God must not be pleased with the Church's failure to respond. He must also be concerned about the Church's silent voice and lack of leadership in addressing this issue. I believe that God strongly wants the Church to provide leadership and guidance to the nation and the world on matters concerning racial injustices and racial healing.

However, before this happens, the sins of prejudice, bigotry, and racism must be addressed by the modern day Church. A good deal of the blame for the negative impact that these spiritual problems have had upon people of color can certainly be placed at the doorstep of the Church. While most churches carry out their "business as usual" agendas, people from diverse racial and cultural backgrounds still continue to be denied apartments, home mortgage loans, home improvement loans, homeowners insurance, employment, business start-up loans, proper medical care, and other public accommodations.

Unfortunately, persons of color are still pulled over by the police in some instances because of the color of their skin and followed in department stores because they are suspected of being potential shoplifters. It is also very difficult to develop new businesses within urban communities because a number of potential sites have been contaminated but not cleaned up due to environmental racism.[2] The number of hate groups continues to grow in the United States and they are now using the Internet to recruit potential members. The most prevalent reason why people are attacked by these groups is because of their race. Also, the National Church Arson Taskforce (NCAT) reported as of July 6, 1999 that within the United States 258 of the church arsons investigated had occurred at African-American churches.[3] The taskforce further reported that 406 of the church arsons occurred in the south, and approximately 180 had occurred at African-American churches.[4]

Racism remains a problem in America and around the globe. This is such a pervasive problem that it demands a serious response from the Church. Several years ago, the cries of racism could be heard when Danny

Glover (a black actor) could not seem to get a taxicab driver to pick him up in New York City, and in Bosnia-Herzegovina where Slobodan Miloservic attempted to exterminate the Serbian people. In Washington, D.C. where the U.S. Supreme Court has came under fire for failing to make an effort to hire racial minorities as law clerks. Once again in New York City, where Armadou Diallo, an African immigrant, was shot at at least forty-one times and killed by the bullets that struck his body nineteen times and in Baltimore, Maryland when the NAACP took major television networks to task for the lack of diversity in the 2000 fall prime-time season line-up.[5] In Greenville, South Carolina, where then Presidential candidate George W. Bush came under fire for giving a speech at Bob Jones University, which originally had a policy on the books that prohibited interracial dating. In Columbia, South Carolina, a great deal of racial animosity erupted over the Confederate flag flying over the Dome of the State house (although the state legislature voted subsequently to take down the flag, many people are still outraged by the legislature's decision to still display the flag elsewhere on the grounds). In Atlanta, Georgia, where Coca-Cola decided in November 2000 to settle a racial discrimination lawsuit for 192.5 million;[6] and also during the same month in the State of Florida, where a large number of black voters alleged that their votes were not counted in the Presidential election.

More recently, we have seen Arab Americans being racially profiled in our country and suspected as largely being terrorists following the terrible events that took place in the United States on September 11, 2001. Charges of racism could be heard in Michigan during the 2002 Gubernatorial race between Republican candidate Dick Posthumous and Democratic candidate Jennifer Granholm when the issue of reparations for descendants of slaves became a campaign issue; and no one could have ever imagined the public condemnation that would be heard throughout the nation when Senate Majority Leader Trent Lott from the state of Mississippi at a 100th birthday tribute for Senator Strom Thurmond stated, " I want to say this about my state: When Strom Thurmond [then a segregationist] ran for president, we voted for him. We're proud of it. And if the rest of the country had followed our lead, we wouldn't have had all these problems over the years."[7] These very controversial remarks made by Senate Majority Leader Trent Lott created such a political firestorm that it eventually led him to resign from his leadership position in the U.S. Senate.

God's Word clearly does not condone the sins of prejudice, bigotry, and racism. However, a large number of pastors across the country will not even address these issues from their pulpits. While so many churches are very generous when it comes to contributing toward missionary work overseas, oftentimes it is very difficult to see the same compassion exhibited in helping to address the inequities of urban communities. Quite frankly, a large number of pastors of non-color would rather run, duck, hide, or bury their heads in the sand than deal with the issues of race and inequality.

Similarly, most churches of non-color that are located within suburban communities have not established significant relationships and/or partnerships with urban churches. As a result of this past neglect, a large number of pastors in the urban community have begun to question the intentions of pastors of non-color from suburban communities when they express an interest in developing a relationship and/or partnership. I have noticed that many persons of non-color enjoy attending wonderful Christian events that call for racial reconciliation but once these events are over they actually do very little to help achieve it. One person of non-color who attended one of these conferences invited me to have lunch with him and apologized to me for his ancestor's involvement with slavery. He even told me that God had placed on his heart that he should stay in touch with me by phone or get together with me on a monthly basis. I have only received two phone calls from this person in seven years since we had lunch. It was from this experience that I discovered what he told me over lunch really did not come from his heart.

This book has not been written to answer any questions regarding to prejudice, bigotry, and racism; but it has been designed to ask a lot of thought-provoking questions that hopefully will produce some life-changing answers. This book will challenge readers that may harbor any prejudice, bigotry, and racism in their hearts to repent, to seek God's forgiveness, and to be restored.

It is my prayer that if any seeds of prejudice, bigotry, or racism have been planted in your heart, God would uncover and expose them by the power of the Holy Spirit as you read this book! Perhaps this book will expose and reveal to you some imperfections of the heart. Please be willing to become vulnerable and transparent before God when you begin to respond to the questions.

Racism is rebellion against a holy and just God and expresses itself individually as well as corporately. Man's rebellion is at the core of a continual drive to be superior, to be in control, to be dependent upon nobody at the expense of others. It is this drive that has brought about the proliferation of all social sin, including oppression, injustice, favoritism (racism) and exploitation.

-Dr. John Perkins, President and author, John M. Perkins Foundation for Reconciliation & Development

While exploring the anatomy of denial is a painstaking task, one thing is clear: denial, in and of itself, isn't a negative psychological reflex, for it springs from a sense of shame—a desire to conceal a feeling that a person knows deep-down is socially incorrect. The thought that ridding one's self of it is an impossibility, encourages more and more repression of the feeling; an action that makes healing more and more difficult—for the deeper the hole, the tougher it is to emerge from it.

- Nathan Rutstein, Author of *Healing Racism in America*

Consider what the Scriptures might offer us. It is readily apparent that the first century did not have a concept of race based on skin color. Yet there were distinctions that brought division and hierarchies that produced discrimination rooted in personal and societal understandings of ethnicity and culture. These differentiations often contained the same emotional and structural force to divide as race does today. This was particularly true of the divide between the Jews and Gentiles. The attempt by many Pharisees to implement an exclusive religion was challenged by the radically-inclusive Jesus. He broke all of the rules that the religious leaders made to separate themselves from others.

- Dr. Michael O. Emerson, Professor and author of *Divided by Faith*

It is oppressive and abusive to convey an ideology that suggests that I will only accept you if you act like me. That is not true love at all. It flows from an arrogant heart that assumes that all we do is right and all that is different from us is wrong.

- Bishop T.D. Jakes, Pastor and Best-selling author, *Woman Thou Art Loosed* and *The Lady, Her Lover and Her Lord*

ONE

QUESTIONS FOR PERSONS
OF NON-COLOR

God's Unconditional Love

■ Do you believe that God loves all people regardless of their racial or cultural background? Why or why not? _____

_____

_____

_____

_____

■ Did you feel that your parents loved persons of color when you were growing up as a child? Why or why not? _____

_____

_____

_____

_____

_____

■ Did you feel your relatives loved persons of color when you were growing up as a child? Why or why not?_____

_____

_____

_____

_____

■ How have your parents' and relatives' feelings about persons of color whether positive or negative affected you? _____

_____

_____

_____

_____

■ Does your spouse love persons of color? Why or why not?

_____

_____

_____

_____

■ How have your spouse's feelings about persons of color whether positive or negative impacted your life?_____

_____

_____

_____

_____

■ Have you taught your children to love all people regardless of their race or cultural background? Why or why not? _____

_____

_____

_____

_____

_____

- Do you love all people regardless of their racial or cultural background? Why or why not?_____

_____

_____

_____

_____

- Do your verbal comments to persons of color on a regular basis indicate that you love them? Why or why not? _____

_____

_____

_____

_____

- Do your actions toward persons of color on a regular basis indicate that you love them? Why or why not? _____

_____

_____

_____

_____

- Do you have any hatred in your heart toward any persons of color? If so, why?_____

_____

_____

_____

_____

- What Bible Scriptures have you read that encourage you to love people from different racial and cultural backgrounds? Please list some of them below:_____

_____

_____

_____

_____

- How have you developed good loving friendships and relationships with persons of color?_____

_____

_____

_____

_____

Media and Entertainment Industry

- How do you feel persons of color are represented by print, radio, cable and television industries? Would you call it negative or positive? Why?_____

_____

_____

_____

_____

- How has the media affected your perceptions about persons of color? Would you call it negative or positive? Why? _____

_____

_____

_____

_____

- How do you feel when you see persons of color being featured in stereotypical roles on television commercials? Does it bother you or not?

_____

_____

_____

_____

- How have television commercials affected your perceptions about persons of color? Would you call it positive or negative? Why?

_____

_____

_____

■ How has the news media (print, radio, cable, television, and Internet) affected your perceptions about persons of color? Would you call it positive or negative? Why?_____

_____

_____

_____

_____

■ How has the television industry in particular affected your perceptions about persons of color? Would you call it positive or negative? Why?

_____

_____

_____

_____

■ How has the motion picture industry affected your perceptions about persons of color? Would you call it positive or negative? Why?

_____

_____

_____

_____

■ How do you feel when you see persons of color depicted in stereo-typical roles in movies that are produced by the motion picture industry? Does it bother you or not? _____

_____

_____

_____

_____

■ How do you feel about persons of color being largely underrepresented in television programming during the prime time lineups by the major television networks and cable networks? Does it bother you or not?

_____

_____

_____

_____

■ How has the recording industry affected your perceptions about persons of color? Would you call it positive or negative? Why? _____

_____

_____

_____

_____

Racial and Cultural Diversity

■ Do you primarily enjoy spending quality time with people who look and act like you? Why or why not? _____

_____

_____

_____

_____

■ How would you feel about inviting a person of color over to your house for dinner? _____

_____

_____

_____

_____

■ Have you ever been invited over to a person of color's house for dinner? When?_____

_____

_____

_____

_____

■ Do you tell stereotypical jokes about persons of color? If yes, why?

_____

_____

_____

_____

- Do you let your friends tell stereotypical jokes about persons of color? If yes, why?_____

_____

_____

_____

_____

- How would you feel about your son or daughter dating a person of color? Would you be comfortable or uncomfortable? Why? _____

_____

_____

_____

_____

- How would you feel about your son or daughter marrying a person of color? Would you be comfortable or uncomfortable? Why?_____

_____

_____

_____

_____

- Would you accept the spouse as a member of your family ? Why or why not? _____

_____

_____

_____

_____

- Would you accept your grandchild if he/she came from an interracial marriage? Why or Why not? _____

_____

_____

_____

_____

_____

- Have you ever treated a person of color differently because of their skin color? Why or why not?_____

_____

_____

_____

_____

- How do you feel when you see a person of color walking toward you at night? Do you feel comfortable or uncomfortable? Why? _____

_____

_____

_____

_____

_____

- What would you do if you saw a person of color walking toward your car? Would you lock your doors? Why or why not? _____

_____

_____

_____

_____

_____

- Do you value spending quality time with persons of color on a regular basis? Why or why not?_____

_____

_____

_____

_____

- Would you value having racial and cultural diversity at your church? Why or why not?_____

_____

_____

_____

_____

- Would you value having racial and cultural diversity at your child's school? Why or why not?_____

_____

_____

_____

- Would you value having racial and cultural diversity at your business or workplace? Why or why not? _____

_____

_____

_____

- Would you value having racial and cultural diversity in your neighborhood? Why or why not? _____

_____

_____

_____

_____

- Do you value what persons of color have to say? Why or why not?

_____

_____

_____

- Do you value the gifts and talents of persons of color? Why or why not? _____

_____

_____

_____

■ Have you taken time to study history and discover what significant contributions persons of color have made? If so, what have you learned from your time of study? _____

_____

_____

_____

_____

■ How do you feel when you go into a room and the majority of people are persons of color? Do you generally feel comfortable or uncomfortable? Why? _____

_____

_____

_____

_____

_____

■ Would you feel more comfortable speaking to a person of non-color or a person of color on a public sidewalk in passing? Why or why not?

_____

_____

_____

_____

■ Do you appreciate what you have in common with people from different racial and cultural backgrounds? Why or why not?

_____

_____

_____

_____

■ Do you appreciate what you do not have in common with people from different racial and cultural backgrounds? Why or why not?

_____

_____

_____

_____

The Church

- Would you prefer to attend a church that primarily consists of persons of non-color or a church that is racially diverse? Why? _____

  _____

  _____

  _____

- How would you feel about attending a church where the persons of color made up the majority of the church members? Would you feel comfortable or uncomfortable? Why?_____

  _____

  _____

  _____

- How would you feel about the topics of prejudice, bigotry, and racism being addressed from the pulpit of your church from a biblical perspective? Would you feel comfortable or uncomfortable? Why?

  _____

  _____

  _____

  _____

- How would you feel about a person of color preaching at your church? Would you be comfortable or uncomfortable? Why? _____

  _____

  _____

  _____

  _____

- Has a person of color ever preached at your church? When? How did you feel about it? Why?_____

  _____

  _____

  _____

  _____

■ How would you feel about persons of color visiting your church on a regular basis? Would you be comfortable or uncomfortable? Why?

_____

_____

_____

■ Why do you believe that a person of color may not want to visit your church? _____

_____

_____

_____

■ How would you feel about persons of color becoming members of your church? Would you be comfortable or uncomfortable? Why?

_____

_____

_____

■ Why do you believe that a person of color may not want to become a member of your church? _____

_____

_____

_____

_____

■ How would you feel about your church reaching out to the urban community? Would you be comfortable or uncomfortable? Why?

_____

_____

_____

_____

■ How would you feel about your church establishing partnerships with churches located in the urban community? Would you be comfortable or uncomfortable? Why?_____

_____

_____

- Has your church established any partnerships with churches located in the urban community? Why or why not? _____

_____

_____

_____

_____

- How would you feel about your church investing significant dollars in the urban community? Would you be comfortable or uncomfortable? Why?_____

_____

_____

_____

_____

- How would you feel about your church sponsoring programs and special events in the urban community? Would you be comfortable or uncomfortable? Why?_____

_____

_____

_____

_____

- How would you feel about your church doing business with some companies owned by persons of color? Would you be comfortable or uncomfortable? Why?_____

_____

_____

_____

_____

- How would you feel about your church using some vendors, suppliers, construction contractors and professional service companies that are owned by persons of color? Would you be comfortable or uncomfortable? Why?_____

_____

_____

■ How would you feel about your church having evangelism programs designed to reach the urban community? Would you be comfortable or uncomfortable? Why?_____

_____

_____

_____

_____

■ What has your church done to help the poor and disadvantaged in your community? Have you been directly involved with such efforts? Why or why not?_____

_____

_____

_____

■ Do you believe that your church staff and the leadership team are sensitive to the needs of persons of color? Why or why not? _____

_____

_____

_____

■ Do you believe that your church and/or denomination's hiring practices would serve as a barrier to persons of color being hired? Why or why not?_____

_____

_____

_____

_____

■ Do you believe that your church and/or denomination's policies and practices seem to be biased toward persons of color? Why or why not?_____

_____

_____

_____

_____

■ Do you believe that your church's programs and special events are designed to effectively reach out to persons of color? Why or why not?

_____

_____

_____

_____

■ Would you prefer to have a church leadership team that consists of persons of non-color or a church leadership team that is racially diverse? Why?_____

_____

_____

_____

■ How would you feel about diverse styles of worship music such as Gospel, Spanish, Jazz, Urban Praise and Worship being incorporated into your church service? Why? _____

_____

_____

_____

_____

■ Have you ever visited a church that primarily consists of persons of color? Why or why not?_____

_____

_____

_____

_____

■ How would you feel about your church sending missionaries to the urban community? Would you be comfortable or uncomfortable? Why?_____

_____

_____

_____

_____

■ How would you feel about your church doing some evangelism or participating in some outreach events in the urban community? Would you be comfortable or uncomfortable? Why? _____

_____

_____

_____

_____

■ Do you believe that the Gospel of Jesus Christ can surpass any racial barriers? Why or why not? _____

_____

_____

_____

_____

■ Do you believe as an ambassador that you can surpass any racial barriers by sharing the gospel of Jesus Christ? Why or why not? _____

_____

_____

_____

_____

■ Have you allowed the spirit of fear to stop you from sharing the gospel in the urban community or overseas on the mission field? Why? _____

_____

_____

_____

_____

■ Do you believe that Jesus died on the cross for everyone? Are you willing to go wherever the Holy Spirit leads you to go and share the gospel? Why or why not? _____

_____

_____

_____

_____

The Business or Workplace

■ Do you believe your employees or coworkers are not sensitive to the needs of persons of color? Why or why not? _____

_____

_____

_____

_____

■ Do you believe that the personnel policies of your business or the company you work for serve as a barrier to persons of color being hired? Why or why not? _____

_____

_____

_____

■ Do you believe that the policies and practices of your business or the company you work for are biased toward persons of color? Why or why not? _____

_____

_____

_____

■ Does your business or the company you work for produce products or provide services that meet the needs of persons of color? Why or why not? _____

_____

_____

_____

■ Does your business or the company you work for ignore the market potential of consumers that come from different racial and cultural backgrounds? Why or why not? _____

_____

_____

_____

_____

■ Does the leadership team of your business or the company you work for consist of persons of non-color? Why or why not? _____

_____

_____

_____

Prejudice, Bigotry, and Racism

■ Have you ever been accused of being prejudiced or bigoted? Why?

_____

_____

_____

_____

■ Have you ever been accused of being a racist? Why? _____

_____

_____

_____

■ Have you ever denied that prejudice and bigotry exists? Why?

_____

_____

_____

_____

■ Have you ever denied that racism exists? Why? _____

_____

_____

_____

■ Have you ever asked any persons of color to tell you about some of their experiences in dealing with prejudice, bigotry and racism? What did you learn from their life experiences? _____

_____

_____

_____

_____

- Have you ever challenged any prejudice, bigotry or racism among your parents, relatives, friends, employees, coworkers, business clients or church members? Why or why not? _____

_____

_____

_____

_____

- Have you ever publicly condemned prejudice, bigotry, and racism? Why or why not? _____

_____

_____

_____

- Have you ever done anything to address prejudice, bigotry, and racism? Why or why not? _____

_____

_____

_____

- What can you do to reach out to persons of color who have been hurt by prejudice, bigotry, and racism? _____

_____

_____

_____

- Have you ever spoken any words or done anything based upon your actions that would be considered to be prejudiced or bigoted? If so, why? _____

_____

_____

_____

- Have you ever spoken any words or done anything based upon your actions that would be considered to be racist? If so, why? _____
  _____
  _____
  _____
  _____

- How do you feel about prejudice and bigotry being viewed as sin in God's eyes? _____
  _____
  _____
  _____
  _____

- How do you feel about racism being viewed as sin in God's eyes?
  _____
  _____
  _____
  _____

- What would you tell God if you had to give account for how you have treated persons of color? Would it be a good or bad report? Why?
  _____
  _____
  _____

- Do you harbor any prejudice or bigotry in your heart? Why or why not?_____
  _____
  _____
  _____

- Do you harbor any racist tendencies in your heart? Why?
  _____
  _____
  _____
  _____

■ What can you do to reach out to persons of non-color who are prejudice, bigoted and racist with the love of Jesus Christ? _____

_____

_____

_____

■ What can you do to reach out to those persons of color that have
been wounded or hurt by prejudice, bigotry and racism?_____

_____

_____

_____

■ How do you feel about God looking at the heart of man rather than
his outward appearance? Does this make you feel comfortable or
uncomfortable? Why?_____

_____

_____

_____

■ Have you ever judged a person of color based upon the color of their
skin? If so, why? _____

_____

_____

_____

■ How do you feel about God's Word proclaiming that people from
every tribe, language, and nation will be in heaven? Why?_____

_____

_____

_____

■ Do you envision a heaven in your mind that is segregated or unsegre-
gated? Why?_____

_____

_____

_____

_____

God's Forgiveness

■ Have you ever been offended by a person of color? When? Why?

_____

_____

_____

_____

■ Have you allowed an offense to impact your feelings or perceptions about persons of color? Why or why not? _____

_____

_____

_____

_____

■ Have you forgiven the person(s) of color that offended you? Why or why not? _____

_____

_____

_____

_____

■ Have you refused to forgive the person(s) of color and as a result are now carrying the weight of the offense on your shoulders? Why?

_____

_____

_____

_____

■ Do you need to ask God to forgive you of the sin of prejudice and/or bigotry? Why or why not?_____

_____

_____

_____

_____

■ Do you need to ask God to forgive you of the sin of racism? Why or why not? _____

_____

_____

_____

_____

What Should We Anticipate in the Future?

■ Did you know that by the year 2050 the U.S. population is expected to grow by 124 million people to an estimated 387 million people? [8] What do you believe will be some contributing factors to the projected growth in U.S. population in the future? _____

_____

_____

_____

_____

■ What do you think of the projection that the white population in the U.S. will shrink to 51 percent by 2050? [9] _____

_____

_____

_____

_____

■ How do you feel about the current population trends that project sometime after the year 2050 the white population will consist of less than half of the U.S. population? [10] _____

_____

_____

_____

_____

■ What do you think of the projection that the black population is expected to increase to 14 percent of the U.S. population by the year 2050?[11] _____

_____

_____

_____

_____

■ What do you think of the projection that the Asian population is expected to increase to 8 percent of the U.S. population by the year 2050?[12] _____

_____

_____

_____

_____

■ What do you think of the projection that the Hispanic population is expected to increase to 26 percent of the U.S. population by the year 2050?[13] _____

_____

_____

_____

■ What do you think about the Hispanic population becoming the largest minority group in the United States according to the 2000 Census?[14] _____

_____

_____

_____

■ What do you think about immigration from Latin America and Asia being the biggest factor affecting changes in the U.S. population?[15] Do you view this as being positive or negative? Why? _____

_____

_____

_____

_____

Casualties of racism have no power because they have given up. Survivors of racism understand that political change can only give us the right to create choices for ourselves, which is the right to take on more burdens individually or as communities, not to pass them off on the government or anyone else. Survivors take ownership of their problems, take inventory of their personal strengths and resources, then use the power within themselves to bring about change.

- Clarence Page, Author of *Showing My Color*

Perhaps the most important idea held in common is that of ridding the society of oppressive domination by one group over another group, together with the related idea of self-determination to the fullest extent possible for every group. With great effort and new imagination in organizing, perhaps this shared vision of a nation free of all such oppression and domination can be used to build successful coalitions in the future.

- Dr. Joe Feagin, Professor and author of *Racist America*

I would rather wait until the racist oppressors have confessed and repented of their sins before I offer them any grace at all. God's grace is already extended to them just as it was extended to me. Each day we need to come alongside God to be forgiven and offer that same forgiveness to those who have sinned against us. What helps me come alongside God is the image of three (not one) crosses on a hill outside Jerusalem. In the middle is Jesus suffering and beside him there are two crucified criminals embodying our response to evil and injustice. On the other side we hold God responsible and demand justice and equity. On the other side we ask for forgiveness and experience God's grace.

- Dr. John Lee, Professor and licensed psychologist, Michigan State University

$\equiv$ Two $\equiv$

Questions for
Persons of Color

God's Unconditional Love

- Do you love persons of non-color? Why or why not?
  _____
  _____
  _____
  _____
  _____

- Do you love people who come from different racial or cultural backgrounds? Why or why not? _____
  _____
  _____
  _____
  _____
  _____

■ How have your parents' feelings about people who come from different racial or cultural backgrounds had an impact on you? Has it been negative or positive? Why? _____

_____

_____

_____

_____

■ How have your relatives' feelings about people who come from different racial or cultural backgrounds had an affect on you? Has it been negative or positive? Why? _____

_____

_____

_____

_____

■ Do you believe that your parents loved persons of non-color when you were growing up as a child? Why or why not? _____

_____

_____

_____

_____

■ How have you parents' feelings about persons of non-color whether positive or negative impacted you? _____

_____

_____

_____

_____

■ Do you feel that your relatives loved persons of non-color when you were growing up as a child? Why or why not? _____

_____

_____

_____

_____

- How have your relatives' feelings about persons of non-color affected you? _____

  _____

  _____

  _____

  _____

- What Bible Scriptures have you read that have encouraged you to love people regardless of their racial or cultural background? _____

  _____

  _____

  _____

  _____

- Have you experienced prejudice and bigotry from persons of non-color? When? What happened?_____

  _____

  _____

  _____

  _____

- How have you been able to heal from any prejudice or bigotry that you may have received from persons of non-color? _____

  _____

  _____

  _____

  _____

- How have you been able to heal from any racism that you may have received from persons of non-color? _____

  _____

  _____

  _____

  _____

■ How have you been able to provide some encouragement to persons of color that have been wounded or hurt by prejudice, bigotry or racism? _____

_____

_____

_____

_____

■ Have you ever experienced prejudice and bigotry from persons of color? When? Why? _____

_____

_____

_____

_____

■ How have you been able to heal from any prejudice and bigotry that you may have received from persons of color?

_____

_____

_____

_____

Racial and Cultural Diversity

■ Would you rather spend quality time with people that come from your racial or cultural background? Why or why not? _____

_____

_____

_____

■ How would you feel about spending quality time with persons who come from different racial or cultural backgrounds? Would you be comfortable or uncomfortable? Why?_____

_____

_____

_____

_____

- How would you feel about inviting a person of non-color over to your house for dinner? _____

  _____
  _____
  _____
  _____

- Have you invited a person of non-color over to your house for dinner? When?_____

  _____
  _____
  _____
  _____

- How would you feel about inviting a person from a different racial or cultural background over to your house for dinner? _____

  _____
  _____
  _____

- Have you ever invited a person from a different racial or cultural background over to your house for dinner? When? _____

  _____
  _____
  _____

- How would you feel about your son or daughter dating a person of non-color? Would you be comfortable or uncomfortable? Why?

  _____
  _____
  _____
  _____

■ How would you feel about your son or daughter dating a person from a different racial or cultural background than your own? Would you be comfortable or uncomfortable? Why? _____

_____

_____

_____

_____

■ How would you feel about your son or daughter marrying a person of non-color? Would you be comfortable or uncomfortable? Why?

_____

_____

_____

_____

■ Would you accept the spouse as a member of your family? Why or why not? _____

_____

_____

_____

■ How would you feel about your son or daughter marrying a person from a different racial or cultural background? Would you be comfortable or uncomfortable? Why? _____

_____

_____

_____

_____

■ Would you accept the spouse as a member of your family? Why or why not? _____

_____

_____

_____

_____

- Would you accept your grandchild if he/she came from an interracial marriage? Why or why not? _____

_____

_____

_____

_____

- How would you feel about being in a room where the majority of the people were persons of non-color? Would you be comfortable or uncomfortable? Why? _____

_____

_____

_____

_____

- What positive experiences have you had with persons of non-color?

_____

_____

_____

_____

_____

- What have you learned from the positive experiences you have had with persons of non-color? _____

_____

_____

_____

_____

- What negative experiences have you had with persons of non-color?

_____

_____

_____

_____

_____

■ What have you learned from any negative experiences that you have had with persons of non-color? _____

_____

_____

_____

_____

■ What positive experiences have you had with people who come from different racial or cultural backgrounds?

_____

_____

_____

_____

■ What have you learned from the positive experiences you have had with people who come from different racial or cultural backgrounds?

_____

_____

_____

_____

■ What negative experiences have you had with people who come from different racial or cultural backgrounds? _____

_____

_____

_____

_____

■ Have you allowed any of the negative experiences to affect your perceptions or feelings about persons that come from a certain racial or cultural background? _____

_____

_____

_____

_____

- What have you learned from the negative experiences you have had with people who come from different racial or cultural backgrounds?

- How have you been able to reach out as an ambassador to persons of non-color that may be prejudiced, bigoted or racist? _____

- How have you been able to reach out as an ambassador to persons of color who have been wounded or hurt as result of being subjected to prejudice, bigotry or racism by persons of non-color? _____

- How have you been able to reach out as an ambassador to persons of color who have been wounded or hurt by people who come from different racial or cultural backgrounds? _____

The Church

- How would you feel about a person of non-color preaching at your church? Would you be comfortable or uncomfortable? Why?

■ Has a person of non-color ever preached at your church? Why or why not? _____

_____

_____

_____

■ Has a person from a different racial or cultural background ever preached at your church? When?_____

_____

_____

_____

_____

■ How would you feel about your church developing some partnerships with churches of non-color? Would you be comfortable or uncomfortable? Why?_____

_____

_____

_____

_____

■ How would you feel about your church developing some partnerships with churches that consist of people who come from different racial or cultural backgrounds? Would you be comfortable or uncomfortable?

_____

_____

_____

_____

■ How would you feel about attending a church that primarily consists of persons of non-color? Would you be comfortable or uncomfortable? Why? _____

_____

_____

_____

■ How would you feel about attending a church that consists of persons from the same racial or cultural background? Would you be comfortable or uncomfortable? Why? _____

_____

_____

_____

_____

■ How would you feel about attending a church that is racially diverse? Would you be comfortable or uncomfortable? Why? _____

_____

_____

_____

_____

■ How would you feel about persons of non-color visiting your church on a regular basis? Would you be comfortable or uncomfortable? Why? _____

_____

_____

_____

_____

■ Do any persons of non-color attend your church on a regular basis?

_____

_____

_____

_____

■ How would you feel about people from different racial or cultural backgrounds visiting your church on a regular basis? Would you be comfortable or uncomfortable? Why? _____

_____

_____

_____

_____

■ How would you feel about people from different racial or cultural backgrounds becoming members of your church? Would you be comfortable or uncomfortable? Why? _____

_____

_____

_____

_____

■ Why would a person of non-color not want to attend your church?

_____

_____

_____

_____

■ Why would a person from a different racial or cultural background not want to attend your church? _____

_____

_____

_____

_____

■ Does your church primarily reach out to people who come from the same racial or cultural background as prospective members? Why?

_____

_____

_____

_____

■ How would you feel about your church reaching out to persons of non-color as prospective members? Would you be comfortable or uncomfortable? Why?_____

_____

_____

_____

_____

■ How would you feel about your church reaching out to persons from different racial or cultural backgrounds as prospective members? Would you be comfortable or uncomfortable? Why?_____

_____

_____

_____

_____

The Business or Workplace

■ Have you encountered any prejudice or bigotry as a business owner or employee? When? Why?_____

_____

_____

_____

_____

■ Have you encountered any racism as a business owner or employee? When? Why? _____

_____

_____

_____

_____

■ How would you feel about persons of non-color being hired at your business or workplace? Why?_____

_____

_____

_____

_____

■ What positive experiences have you had working with persons of non-color? _____

_____

_____

_____

_____

- What negative experiences have you had working with persons of non-color? _____

_____

_____

_____

- What have you learned based upon the positive or negative experiences that you have had working with persons of non-color?

_____

_____

_____

_____

- How would you feel about people from different racial or cultural backgrounds being hired at your business or workplace? Why?

_____

_____

_____

_____

- What positive experiences have you had working with people from different racial or cultural backgrounds? _____

_____

_____

_____

- What negative experiences have you had working with people from different racial or cultural backgrounds?_____

_____

_____

_____

- What have you learned based upon the positive or negative experiences that you have had working with people from different racial or cultural backgrounds? _____

_____

_____

- Do people from diverse racial and cultural backgrounds at your business or workplace get along? If not, what can be done to improve your work environment? _____

_____

_____

_____

_____

- Have you ever been denied an employment position or a promotion because of your race or cultural background? When? _____

_____

_____

_____

_____

- Have you ever been denied a business loan because of your racial or cultural background? When? _____

_____

_____

_____

_____

- Have you taken a stand against prejudice, bigotry, and racism at your business or workplace? Why or why not?_____

_____

_____

_____

_____

- Do you value having racial and cultural diversity at your business or in the workplace? Why?_____

_____

_____

_____

_____

_____

■ Does your business or the company you work for have a racially diverse management team? Why? or Why not?_____

_____

_____

_____

_____

■ How have you as a business owner or an employee been able to heal from being wounded or hurt by any prejudice or bigotry? _____

_____

_____

_____

_____

■ How have you as a business owner or an employee been able to heal from being wounded or hurt by any racism? _____

_____

_____

_____

_____

Forgiveness

■ Have you forgiven persons of non-color that may have treated you badly because of your race or cultural background? When? Why?

_____

_____

_____

_____

■ Have you forgiven persons of non-color that may have treated your parents, relatives or ancestors badly because of their race or cultural background? When? Why?_____

_____

_____

_____

_____

- Have you forgiven persons of non-color for any racist behavior that they may have directed toward your parents, relatives or ancestors? When? Why? _____

  _____

  _____

  _____

- Have you forgiven any persons of color that may have treated you badly because of your race or cultural background? When? Why?

  _____

  _____

  _____

  _____

- Have you ever felt like taking revenge against the persons of non-color that may have treated you badly because of your race or cultural background? When? Why? _____

  _____

  _____

  _____

  _____

- Have you ever felt like taking revenge against persons of non-color that may have treated your parents, relatives or ancestors badly because of their racial or cultural background? When? Why? _____

  _____

  _____

  _____

  _____

- Have you ever felt like taking revenge against persons of color that may have treated you badly because of your racial or cultural background? When? Why? _____

  _____

  _____

  _____

■ Have you ever felt like taking revenge against the persons of color that may have treated your parents, relatives and ancestors badly because of their racial or cultural background? When? Why?

_____

_____

_____

_____

■ Do you need to ask God to forgive you and repent for having an unforgiving heart?_____

_____

_____

_____

_____

Three

Photographs and Questions

Please take a few moments to review the following photographs and respond to some questions.

- Do you have any close friends that come from this racial or cultural background?_____
  _____
  _____
  _____

- How did your family's verbal comments or actions towards persons from this racial or cultural background affect you? _____
  _____
  _____
  _____
  _____

- How have you treated people that come from this racial or cultural background?_____

_____

_____

_____

_____

- Do you need to ask God to forgive you for any negative comments or wrongful actions toward people that come from this racial background?_____

_____

_____

_____

_____

- Do you need to make restitution to any people that come from this racial or cultural background because of the way you have treated them?_____

_____

_____

_____

_____

- Do you have any close friends that come from this racial or cultural background?_____

_____

_____

_____

- How did your family's verbal comments or actions towards persons from this racial or cultural background affect you?

_____

_____

_____

_____

- How have you treated people that come from this racial or cultural background?_____

_____

_____

_____

_____

■ Do you need to ask God to forgive you for any negative comments or wrongful actions toward people that come from this racial or cultural background?_____

_____

_____

_____

■ Do you need to make restitution to any people that come from this racial or cultural background because of the way you have treated them?_____

_____

_____

_____

■ Do you have any close friends that come from this racial or cultural background?_____

_____

_____

■ How did your family's verbal comments or actions towards persons from this racial or cultural affect you? _____

_____

_____

_____

■ How have you treated people that come from this racial or cultural background?_____

_____

_____

■ Do you need to ask God to forgive you for any negative comments or wrongful actions toward people that come from this racial or cultural background?_____

_____

_____

■ Do you need to make restitution to any people that come from this racial or cultural background because of the way you have treated them?_____

_____

_____

_____

_____

■ Do you have any close friends that come from this racial or cultural background?_____

_____

_____

_____

■ How did your family's verbal comments or actions towards persons from this racial or cultural background affect you? _____

_____

_____

_____

_____

■ How have you treated people that come from this racial or cultural background?_____

_____

_____

_____

_____

- Do you need to ask God to forgive you for any negative comments or wrongful actions toward people that come from this racial or cultural background?_____

_____

_____

_____

- Do you need to make restitution to any people that come from this racial or cultural background because of the way you have treated them?

_____

_____

_____

_____

■ Do you have any close friends that come from this ethnic group?

_____

_____

_____

_____

■ How did your family's verbal comments or actions towards persons from this ethnic group affect you? _____

_____

_____

_____

_____

■ How have you treated people that come from this ethnic group?

_____

_____

_____

_____

_____

_____

■ Do you need to ask God to forgive you for any negative comments or wrongful actions toward people that come from this particular ethnic group?_____

_____

_____

_____

■ Do you need to make restitution to any people that come from this ethnic group because of the way you have treated them? _____

_____

_____

_____

_____

Special Note: According to the United States Equal Opportunity Commission, Hispanic/Latino is characterized by the U.S. government as an ethnicity because people of Hispanic or Latino origin can be of any race.

Photograph by Michael Morin

■ Do you have any close friends that come from this racial or cultural background?_____

_____

_____

_____

_____

■ How did your family's verbal comments or actions towards persons from this racial or cultural background affect you? _____

_____

_____

_____

_____

■ How have you treated people that come from this racial or cultural background?_____

_____

_____

_____

_____

■ Do you need to ask God to forgive you for any negative comments or wrongful actions toward people that come from this racial or cultural background?_____

_____

_____

_____

■ Do you need to make restitution to any people that come from this racial or cultural background because of the way you have treated them?_____

_____

_____

_____

Four

The Bible and Racism

While there seems to be a gulf between our own understanding of racism and the type of racism that occurred during biblical times, it existed then and is still alive and well today. Although the words race or racism cannot be found in the Bible, the devil has used prejudice, bigotry, and racism as powerful spiritual weapons to divide people. During the time that the Gospel was being written, people were very much divided by race, culture, education, religion, socioeconomic status, and language barriers. Unfortunately, these same barriers exist today, and, to a large extent, are much more prevalent.

We must look to God's Word to discover how we can break through the barriers that the devil has used to create divisions among people. Unfortunately, he is still using these spiritual weapons today to divide people throughout the world and the Church.

Please take a few moments and read the following ten devotionals and you will discover how you can capture God's heart for racial and cultural diversity:

Jesus and the Samaritan Woman:

Do you take paths that lead toward people who come from diverse racial and cultural backgrounds or away from them?

The Pharisees heard that Jesus was gaining and baptizing more disciples than John, although in fact it was not Jesus who baptized, but his disciples. When the Lord learned of this, he left Judea and went back once more to Galilee.

Now he had to go through Samaria. So he came to a town in Samaria called Sychar near the plot of ground Jacob had given to his son Joseph. Jacob's well was there, and Jesus, tired as he was from the journey, sat down by the well. It was about the sixth hour.

When a Samaritan woman came to draw water, Jesus said to her, "Will you give me a drink?" (His disciples had gone into the town to buy food.)

The Samaritan woman said to him, "You are a Jew and I am a Samaritan woman. How can you ask me for a drink?" (For Jews do not associate with Samaritans.)

Jesus answered her, "If you knew the gift of God and who it is that asks you for a drink, you would have asked him and he would have given you living water."

"Sir," the woman said, "you have nothing to draw with and the well is deep. Where can you get this living water? Are you greater than our father Jacob, who gave us the well and drank from it himself, as did also his sons and his flocks and herds?"

Jesus answered, "Everyone who drinks this water will be thirsty again, but whoever drinks the water I give him will never thirst. Indeed, the water I give him will become in him a spring of water welling up to eternal life."

The woman said to him, "Sir, give me this water so that I won't get thirsty and have to keep coming here to draw water."

He told her, "Go, call your husband, and come back."

"I have no husband," she replied.

Jesus said to her, "You are right when you say you have no husband. The fact is, you have had five husbands, and the man you now have is not your husband. What you have just said is quite true."

"Sir," the woman said, "I can see that you are a prophet. Our fathers worshiped on this mountain, but you Jews claim that the place where we must worship is in Jerusalem."

Jesus declared, "Believe me, woman, a time is coming when you will worship the Father neither on this mountain nor in Jerusalem. You Samaritans worship what you do not know; we worship what we do know, for salvation is from the Jews. Yet a time is coming and has now come when the true worshipers will worship the Father in spirit and truth, for they are the kind of worshipers the Father seeks. God is spirit, and His worshipers must worship in spirit and in truth."

The woman said, "I know that Messiah" (called Christ) "is coming. When he comes, he will explain everything to us." Then Jesus declared, "I who speak to you am he."

John 4:1-26

Observations

You will never be able to become an advocate for racial unity or racial justice by seeking to avoid having any human contact or interaction with people who come from different racial and cultural backgrounds. God's Word will always challenge you to give away the love of Jesus Christ by walking toward people rather than away from people. Have you ever walked away from someone who was different from you? Why? How often have you chosen to take a road directly into the life of a person that comes from a different racial or cultural background?

The Book of John reveals in Chapter 4:4 that Jesus had to "go through Samaria." The Savior chose to take a route directly through Samaria rather than avoiding the city altogether, as did most Jews who desired not to come into contact with the Samaritans. Most Jews, as a result of their own prejudices toward the Samaritan people, chose to take a six day journey in order to avoid Samaria rather than taking a three day journey by going directly through the city. The Jews hated the Samaritans because they considered them to be half-breeds—not genuine Jews because their bloodlines were no longer pure—they had chosen to marry people who were not of the Jewish race.

Jesus had a powerful encounter with the Samaritan woman at Jacob's well that would forever change her destiny because He chose not to avoid Samaria. The Samaritan woman would have never had a life-changing encounter with the Savior if He would have allowed the racial prejudice of His own fellow Jews to influence His words and actions. Jesus decided to break through the prejudices of His own people by going directly through Samaria and speaking into the Samaritan woman's life.

Jesus sparked conversation with the Samaritan woman at the well by asking her for a drink of water. The woman must have been completely startled by her encounter with Jesus' because she knew that the Samaritans (her people) and Jews (His people) generally had no dealings with one another. She immediately responded to Jesus' request by attempting to build a wall of separation between them that was based upon racial prejudice. We will never be able to achieve racial unity as long as we allow our racial or cultural differences to get in the way of us coming together in unity based upon what Jesus Christ did for us on the cross.

Jesus spoke directly into the Samaritan woman's life, and it completely changed her destiny. This particular woman had been trying to find peace, joy, and happiness through her relationships with men. However, Jesus offered her far more; He offered her living water, the type of water where she would never thirst again. This Samaritan woman's life would never be the same again, because she finally found the genuine peace that she been searching for but could not find prior to her having an encounter with the Savior. Many Samaritans came to know Jesus as their Messiah as a result of the Samaritan woman sharing her powerful testimony with them. When was the last time that you were able to break through any racial barriers and speak directly into a person's life?

Personal Reflections

■ Please take a few moments and write down your initial reactions or thoughts concerning the scriptural passage._____

_____

_____

_____

_____

_____

_____

_____

_____

■ Please take a few moments and write down what further insight you were able to gain from the scriptural passage as a result of reading the author's observation._____

_____

_____

_____

_____

_____

_____

_____

■ How do you intend to take the scriptural passage and what further information you obtained from reading the commentary and apply it to your life?_____

_____

_____

_____

_____

_____

_____

Philip and the Ethiopian:

Do you allow God's Spirit to show you where to go and share the Gospel and to whom you need to share its life-changing message with?

Now an angel of the Lord said to Philip, "Go south to the road—the desert road-that goes down from Jerusalem to Gaza." So he started out, and on his way he met an Ethiopian eunuch, an important official in charge of all the treasury of Candace, queen of the Ethiopians. This man had gone to Jerusalem to worship, and on his way home was sitting in his chariot reading the book of Isaiah the prophet. The Spirit told Philip, "Go to that chariot and stay near it."

Then Philip ran up to the chariot and heard the man reading Isaiah the prophet. "Do you understand what you are reading?" Philip asked.

"How can I," he said, "unless someone explains it to me?" So he invited Philip to come up and sit with him.

The eunuch was reading this passage of Scripture:

"He was led like a sheep to the slaughter, and as a lamb before the shearer is silent, so he did not open his mouth. In his humiliation he was deprived of justice. Who can speak of his descendants? For his life was taken from the earth."

The eunuch asked Philip, "Tell me, please, who is the prophet talking about, himself or someone else?" Then Philip began with that very passage of Scripture and told him the good news about Jesus.

As they traveled along the road, they came to some water and the eunuch said, "Look, here is water. Why shouldn't I be baptized?" And he gave orders to stop the chariot. Then both Philip and the eunuch went down into the water and Philip baptized him. When they came up out of the water, the Spirit of the Lord suddenly took Philip away, and the eunuch did not see him again, but went on his way rejoicing. Philip, however, appeared at Azotus and traveled about, preaching the Gospel in all the towns until he reached Caesarea.

Acts 8:26-40

Observations

Philip allowed God to direct him to where he needed to go to share the Gospel message. He also allowed the Holy Spirit to direct him to the Ethiopian eunuch that definitely needed a revelation of Jesus Christ, the Messiah. Do you allow God on a regular basis to show you where you need to go to share the Gospel? Do you allow the Holy Spirit to lead you to the person(s) that desperately need to hear the Gospel message? Some believers have not been very effective at sharing the Gospel because they have failed to correctly answer the above questions.

A heart filled with hatred can hinder the Gospel message from being shared with unbelievers. Sadly, many believers have never examined their own hearts concerning prejudice, bigotry and racism. Many believers walk around doing some wonderful things for the kingdom but their hearts are filled with hatred toward persons of color. Either these believers hearts have been so deceived by the devil into thinking that they are "spiritually fit" when they are really sick spiritually, or worse yet, some of these believers are familiar with Jesus but they don't really know Him.

Unfortunately, some persons of non-color that are believers are unable to reach out and share the Gospel with persons of color because they are prejudice toward them. Many believers simply do not feel comfortable sharing the Gospel in urban communities or mission fields overseas where a majority of the people consists of persons of color. In certain instances, these believers have become so fearful because they have seen persons of color and minority neighborhoods depicted so negatively by the secular media (print, television, and radio) that they refuse to reach out with the love of Jesus Christ. Many of these people are simply afraid of being robbed, physically injured or killed if they extend a loving hand. God is looking for modern day Philips that will take the Gospel to places where others would rather not go and reach out to people that society would simply like to discard and forget about. Do you have the desire to go to an urban community or mission field overseas where the majority of the nation consists of persons of color to share the Gospel? Have you refused to go because you are afraid?

Philip was told by the Spirit of God to go and stand near the chariot. If we are going to be effective witnesses for the Kingdom then we must be willing to go to the people rather than simply expecting them to come to us. Philip got so close to the chariot where he was able to hear the Ethiopian eunuch reading Scripture from the book of Isaiah. We should no longer expect unchurched people to simply show up at our church buildings in large numbers anymore. Therefore, the only way that we can get close enough to reach unbelievers is to go directly to them. Philip got so close to the Ethiopian's chariot where he was able to strike up conversation with him by asking a question. The right question posed at the right time can begin to break up the shallow ground of an unbeliever's heart where he may be receptive to hearing the Gospel. Philip discovered by asking the Ethiopian eunuch a question that he lacked an understanding of the scriptural passage that he was reading from the Book of Isaiah.

Philip spoke something into the Ethiopian's life that gave him a profound revelation that Jesus Christ was more than a prophet; He was the Messiah! When was the last time that you spoke into a person's life where he gained a better understanding of God's Word? There are people that we walk past each day that have never accepted Jesus Christ as their personal Savior. Philip was able to deposit something into the Ethiopian's life that would forever change his destiny. Can you imagine how different the outcome would have been if Philip would have chosen to run away from the chariot rather than directly toward it?

God completely orchestrated Philip's encounter with the Ethiopian for a divine purpose. Once God's purpose for this meeting had been accomplished, the Bible tells us that "the Spirit of the Lord suddenly took Philip away." Although the Bible does not provide us with any further information on the Ethiopian eunuch following his encounter with Philip, some scholars have suggested that he probably played a significant role in the Gospel being spread in his own city and throughout the nation of Africa.

Personal Reflections

■ Please take a few moments and write down your initial reactions or thoughts concerning the scriptural passage. _____

_____

_____

_____

_____

_____

_____

_____

_____

■ Please take a few moments and write down what further insight you were able to gain from the scriptural passage as a result of reading the author's observation. _____

_____

_____

_____

_____

_____

_____

_____

■ How do you intend to take the scriptural passage and what further information you obtained from reading the commentary and apply it to your life? _____

_____

_____

_____

_____

_____

_____

The Problem: Moses' Interracial Marriage:

Would you allow your son or daughter to date or marry a person from a different racial or cultural background?

Miriam and Aaron began to talk against Moses because of his Cushite wife, for he had married a Cushite. "Has the Lord spoken only through Moses?" they asked. "Hasn't he also spoken through us?" And the Lord heard this.

(Now Moses was a very humble man, more humble than anyone else on the face of the earth.)

At once the Lord said to Moses, Aaron and Miriam, "Come out to the Tent of Meeting, all three of you." So the three of them came out. Then the Lord came down in a pillar of cloud; He stood at the entrance to the tent and summoned Aaron and Miriam. When both of them stepped forward, He said, "Listen to my words: When a prophet of the Lord is among you, I reveal Myself to him in visions, I speak to him in dreams. But this is not true of my servant Moses; he is faithful in all My house. With him I speak face to face, clearly and not in riddles; he sees the form of the Lord. Why then were you not afraid to speak against my servant Moses?"

The anger of the Lord burned against them, and he left them.

When the cloud lifted from above the Tent, there stood Miriam—leprous, like snow. Aaron turned toward her and saw that she had leprosy; and he said to Moses, "Please, my lord, do not hold against us the sin we have so foolishly committed. Do not let her be like a stillborn infant coming from its mother's womb with its flesh half eaten away."

So Moses cried out to the Lord, "O God, please heal her!"

The Lord replied to Moses, "If her father had spit in her face, would she not have been in disgrace for seven days? Confine her outside the camp for seven days; after that she can be brought back." So Miriam was confined outside the camp for seven days, and the people did not move on till she was brought back.

After that, the people left Hazeroth and encamped in the Desert of Paran.

Numbers 12:1-6

Observations

God's Word makes it clear in the above passage of Scripture that Miriam and Aaron had a problem with Moses' Cushite wife. To put it another way, they had a problem with race of Moses' wife. Many scholars tend to downplay or try to sweep under the carpet the fact that Miriam and Aaron had a problem with Moses' interracial marriage. The Bible clearly indicates in Numbers 12 that this was the reason they began to talk about Moses behind his back. Most scholars for some reason want to spend more time focusing attention on Miriam and Aaron's lack of respect for the position of authority that Moses held and how jealous they were over his close relationship with God. We can obviously arrive a different interpretation of Scripture by trying to make one sin much bigger than another, because God does not put our sins on a scale and comparatively weigh them against each other; in God's eyes, whenever we commit a sin, it is still sin. Miriam and Aaron's reaction to Moses' wife being a Cushite was just as sinful as their lack of respect and jealousy over his close relationship with God.

God chose to deal with the sin in the camp right away. He called for all of the parties involved with the matter to come out of the tent. Therefore, Moses, Miriam, and Aaron came out. Then God descended in a pillar of cloud; stood at the entrance of the tent and had the two individuals that sinned against Him step forward. As a result, Miriam and Aaron both stepped forward. God spoke with them about the special relationship He only had with Moses and then asked them why they chose to speak against Moses.

The incident that took place reveals how God does not have any patience or tolerance for racial prejudice being directed against people or for anyone that shows a lack of respect for those who serve in positions of authority. God's anger, the Bible tells us, burned against Miriam and Aaron, and then He departed. Miriam was found to have leprosy once God had left their presence.

There are several lessons that can be learned from the encounter that God had with Moses, Miriam, and Aaron outside the tent. Number one: God's anger will burn against anyone who uses racial prejudice as a spiritual weapon against persons of color or those who a show a lack of respect for people that God has placed in positions of leadership.

Number two: God will have nothing to do with our sin; this is the reason why He immediately left the camp after He had Miriam and Aaron step forward as a result of their sin. Number three: God will always deal with sin in the camp. When Aaron turned around and saw that Miriam had leprosy, he immediately pleaded with Moses to not count the sin against her. Moses interceded on Miriam's behalf and asked God to heal her. God instructed Moses to take Miriam outside the camp for seven days and then bring her back to the camp. This is simply a good reminder that there are always consequences to sin. What makes this Bible story so powerful is that God was still willing to have mercy on Miriam and Aaron despite their sin. God provided a complete healing to Miriam's body in seven days, and He also spared her life.

Do you have a problem with interracial dating? Do you have a problem with interracial marriages? Do you have any problems with children who come from interracial marriages? Did you know that there is nothing that can be found in God's Word that forbids interracial dating or interracial marriages? Did you know that the only thing that God does not condone concerning marriage is for unbelievers to be unequally yoked in marriage with unbelievers? Have you shown a lack of respect for any person that God has placed in a position of authority over you? Do you need to ask God to forgive you and repent of any sin based upon how you responded to the above questions?

Personal Reflections

- Please take a few moments and write down your initial reactions or thoughts concerning the scriptural passage._____

  _____

  _____

  _____

  _____

  _____

  _____

  _____

- Please take a few moments and write down what further insight you were able to gain from the scriptural passage as a result of reading the author's observation. _____

  _____

  _____

  _____

  _____

  _____

  _____

  _____

- How do you intend to take the scriptural passage and what further information you obtained from reading the commentary and apply it to your life? _____

  _____

  _____

  _____

  _____

  _____

  _____

The Good Samaritan Goes Beyond Racial Barriers:

*Would you stop to help a person in need or would you
simply pass by and keep on going?*

On one occasion an expert in the law stood up to test Jesus. "Teacher," he asked, "what must I do to inherit eternal life?"

"What is written in the Law?" he replied. "How do you read it?"

He answered: " 'Love the Lord your God with all your heart and with all your soul and with all your strength and with all your mind'; and, 'Love your neighbor as yourself.'"

"You have answered correctly," Jesus replied. "Do this and you will live."

But he wanted to justify himself, so he asked Jesus, "And who is my neighbor?"

In reply Jesus said: "A man was going down from Jerusalem to Jericho, when he fell into the hands of robbers. They stripped him of his clothes, beat him and went away, leaving him half dead. A priest happened to be going down the same road, and when he saw the man, he passed by on the other side. So too, a Levite, when he came to the place and saw him, passed by on the other side. But a Samaritan, as he traveled, came where the man was; and when he saw him, he took pity on him. He went to him and bandaged his wounds, pouring on oil and wine. Then he put the man on his own donkey, took him to an inn and took care of him. The next day he took out two silver coins and gave them to the innkeeper. 'Look after him,' he said, 'and when I return, I will reimburse you for any extra expense you may have.'"

Luke 10:25-37

Observations

Jesus had a powerful encounter with a religious leader in Luke 10. This particular teacher of the law wanted to test Jesus by asking what he must do to inherit eternal life. Rather than answer the question, Jesus instead decided to ask the teacher two questions. Number one: He asked him what the law said regarding this matter; and Number two: He asked the teacher to give Him his interpretation of what the law said. The teacher responded to Jesus' questions by reciting Deuteronomy 6:5. Jesus answered by telling the teacher that he responded correctly to His question and instructed him to live his life according to what the law said regarding the matter. Rather than simply be satisfied with what Jesus told him, the teacher sought to gain the upper hand by asking the Savior one more question.

Jesus decided not to respond to the teacher's question but instead he began to talk about the parable of the Good Samaritan. He simply chose to talk about the parable and to let the teacher discover the biblical truth behind the lesson that he was trying to teach him. The teacher asked the question with the intent of trying to get Jesus to agree that his neighbors were his fellow Jews. However, Jesus chose to tell him a parable about how the Good Samaritan was able to break through the racial barriers that separated Jews from Samaritans.

Jesus explained this parable to the teacher of the law by telling him about a Jewish man who took a trip from Jerusalem to Jericho and was robbed. The man had been stripped of his clothes, beaten, and left for dead. Jesus revealed in the parable that a priest (Jewish religious leader) and Levite encountered this man but refused to help him and crossed the street so they could avoid having any contact with him. What is very interesting about this parable is that the most unlikely person (the Samaritan) stopped to help the Jewish man who was in desperate need of help.

Can you imagine how very difficult this parable must have been for the teacher to listen to at the time? Jews hated the Samaritans; they were considered to half-breeds in their eyes. Also, they had significant differences that kept them apart that were based upon religion. The teacher was probably waiting with great anticipation for Jesus to tell him that the Jewish priest had stopped to help a fellow Jew who needed help. He also probably made the assumption that neither the Levite or the Samaritan would stop at all to provide any help. However, it was the Good Samaritan that chose to break through the racial and religious barriers of his day by stopping to help the Jewish man.

What is very interesting about this parable is the Samaritan went beyond the call of duty in an effort to provide assistance. He did not simply stop to help the Jewish man for a few moments; he went out of his way to help him. The Samaritan bandaged his wounds, transported him to the inn, took care of him overnight, paid for his lodging, requested that the innkeeper take care of him during his absence, and offered to take care of any additional expenses incurred once he returned. Do you remember the last time that you stopped to help someone in need? Did you go way beyond the call of duty to help the person in need? Have you ever refused to help a person based upon their racial or cultural background, socioeconomic status or the neighborhood where they live?

Personal Reflections

■ Please take a few moments and write down your initial reactions or thoughts concerning the scriptural passage. _____

_____

_____

_____

_____

_____

_____

_____

_____

■ Please take a few moments and write down what further insight you were able to gain from the scriptural passage as a result of reading the author's observation. _____

_____

_____

_____

_____

_____

_____

_____

■ How do you intend to take the scriptural passage and what further information you obtained from reading the commentary and apply it to your life? _____

_____

_____

_____

_____

_____

_____

_____

Paul Challenges Peter's Prejudice:

Do you tell people that you love them while your actions toward them communicate an entirely different message?

When Peter came to Antioch, I opposed him to his face, because he was clearly in the wrong. Before certain men came from James, he used to eat with the Gentiles. But when they arrived, he began to draw back and separate himself from the Gentiles because he was afraid of those who belonged to the circumcision group. The other Jews joined him in his hypocrisy, so that by their hypocrisy even Barnabas was led astray.

When I saw that they were not acting in line with the truth of the Gospel, I said to Peter in front of them all, "You are a Jew, yet you live like a Gentile and not like a Jew. How is it, then, that you force Gentiles to follow Jewish customs?

"We who are Jews by birth and not 'Gentile sinners' know that a man is not justified by observing the law, but by faith in Jesus Christ. So we, too, have put our faith in Christ Jesus that we may be justified by faith in Christ and not by observing the law, because by observing the law no one will be justified.

"If, while we seek to be justified in Christ, it becomes evident that we ourselves are sinners, does that mean that Christ promotes sin? Absolutely not! If I rebuild what I destroyed, I prove that I am a lawbreaker. For through the law I died to the law so that I might live for God. I have been crucified with Christ and I no longer live, but Christ lives in me. The life I live in the body, I live by faith in the Son of God, who loved me and gave himself for me. I do not set aside the grace of God, for if righteousness could be gained through the law, Christ died for nothing!"

Galatians 2:11-21

Observations

Paul confronted Peter over his prejudicial behavior toward the Gentiles. God's Word tells us that Paul went directly to Peter to have an intense conversation with him about his behavior. Paul noticed that Peter had begun to withdraw and separate himself from the Gentiles because he was concerned about how the Judaizers (these were Jews that felt based upon the law that all Gentiles needed to be circumcised) would perceive his actions. Peter's prejudicial behavior toward the Gentiles sent a clear message to his fellow Jews and to Barnabas that such behavior was acceptable.

What is ironic about Peter's actions toward the Gentiles is that he engaged in this prejudicial behavior after God had given him a vision about the four-footed animals both clean and unclean (Acts 10:9-48). Peter's actions toward the Gentiles were contrary to the understanding and insight about the vision that he received at Cornelius' house! He made the following two statements after he received the revelation and understanding of the vision that was given to him by the Holy Spirit:

"You are well aware that it is against our law for a Jew to associate with a Gentile or visit him. But God has shown me that I should not call any man impure or unclean. So when I was sent for, I came without raising any objection" (Acts 10:28-29).

"I now realize how true it is that God does not show favoritism but accepts men from every nation who fear him and do what is right" (Acts 10:34).

Peter had begun to have dinner with Jews and Gentiles while he was in Antioch after God had given him such a powerful vision and interpretation of its message. However, when he arrived in Jerusalem, he did not continue the walk in the same spirit of unity that he did in Antioch. Peter had begun to revert back to his old prejudicial behavior that prevented Jews and Gentiles from having fellowship and dining together. Paul strongly rebuked Peter publicly in front of everyone for his unacceptable behavior by asking him a rhetorical question. He basically asked Peter why he was trying to force Gentiles to live by Jewish customs when as a Jew he himself did not even live according to the same standards. Paul was clearly justified by calling Peter on the carpet for preaching a message of a salvation in Christ that was available for everyone but engaging in prejudicial behavior that would not create a spirit of unity but one of division.

There are many lessons that can be learned from Paul's public rebuke of Peter for his racial prejudice. Number one: As believers we always need to confront prejudice, bigotry and racism regardless of the consequences. Number two: We cannot tell people we love them but communicate a message that does not represent the love of Jesus Christ based upon our word or actions. Number three: We should always desire to walk in the Spirit rather than the flesh so we will not want to return to or embrace our old sin nature. Number four: We should never compromise our Christian beliefs in order to be accepted or fit in with the crowd. Number five: We should never underestimate to what extent people may be influenced by our words or actions. Number six: We should always remember that God does not mind correcting or humbling us in public whenever we choose to flaunt our sin before people.

Personal Reflections

■ Please take a few moments and write down your initial reactions or thoughts concerning the scriptural passage. _____

_____

_____

_____

_____

_____

_____

_____

_____

■ Please take a few moments and write down what further insight you were able to gain from the scriptural passage as a result of reading the author's observation._____

_____

_____

_____

_____

_____

_____

_____

■ How do you intend to take the scriptural passage and what further information you obtained from reading the commentary and apply it to your life?_____

_____

_____

_____

_____

_____

_____

_____

James Discourages Favoritism:

Do you show favoritism toward certain people?

My brothers, as believers in our glorious Lord Jesus Christ, don't show favoritism. Suppose a man comes into your meeting wearing a gold ring and fine clothes, and a poor man in shabby clothes also comes in. If you show special attention to the man wearing fine clothes and say, "Here's a good seat for you," but say to the poor man, "You stand there" or "Sit on the floor by my feet," have you not discriminated among yourselves and become judges with evil thoughts?

Listen, my dear brothers: Has not God chosen those who are poor in the eyes of the world to be rich in faith and to inherit the Kingdom he promised those who love him? But you have insulted the poor. Is it not the rich who are exploiting you? Are they not the ones who are dragging you into court? Are they not the ones who are slandering the noble name of him to whom you belong? If you really keep the royal law found in Scripture, "Love your neighbor as yourself," you are doing right. But if you show favoritism, you sin and are convicted by the law as lawbreakers.

For whoever keeps the whole law and yet stumbles at just one point is guilty of breaking all of it. For he who said, "Do not commit adultery," also said, "Do not murder." If you do not commit adultery but do commit murder, you have become a lawbreaker.

Speak and act as those who are going to be judged by the law that gives freedom, because judgment without mercy will be shown to anyone who has not been merciful. Mercy triumphs over judgment!

James 2:1-12

Observations

James strongly encouraged his fellow believers to not show favoritism toward one another. How often have you judged a person based upon the type of car they drive, where they live, the type of clothes they wear, the type of job they have, the color of their skin, their educational background, or their socioeconomic status? James became concerned about the problem of favoritism among believers when he noticed that they were treating some people different from others. When a person shows favoritism toward another person, then they have denied him the right to have something. James strongly admonishes believers to not show favoritism and therefore discriminate against one another. James 2:4 reveals that when a person shows favoritism they "become judges with evil thoughts." How often have you passed judgment on a person that has crossed your path?

James was not addressing the secular world when he spoke out against favoritism. He was addressing believers that make up the Church. How many people has God sent across your path that could do great things for the Kingdom, but much like the world does, you simply pass by them or avoided them altogether? How often have you wanted to get to know someone who had money, power, and influence? How often, in comparison, have you wanted to get to know a person who would be considered to be poor or disadvantaged?

God often calls the least likely people to do great things for the Kingdom. We need to put on spiritual lenses so we can see the God potential in others. When we begin to do this, then we will see the God potential in an urban child who comes from a disadvantaged background, or the single mother who is desperately trying to make enough money to raise her children, or the homeless person who stays at a rescue mission, or the prostitute that was physically and sexually abused as a child who now stands on the corner waiting for the next car to stop, or the gang member who came from a broken home without receiving genuine love from his mother or father, or the inmate that is presently behind bars serving time for a crime he committed. When a person really loves someone, then he will not discriminate or treat the individual differently. The Bible clearly indicates that whenever a believer chooses to show favoritism toward another person then he has chosen to sin and be disobedient to God. Have you been showing favoritism toward certain people? Do you need to repent and ask God to forgive you for showing favoritism toward people?

Personal Reflections

■ Please take a few moments and write down your initial reactions or thoughts concerning the scriptural passage._____

_____

_____

_____

_____

_____

_____

_____

_____

_____

■ Please take a few moments and write down what further insight you were able to gain from the scriptural passage as a result of reading the author's observation._____

_____

_____

_____

_____

_____

_____

■ How do you intend to take the scriptural passage and what further information you obtained from reading the commentary and apply it to your life? _____

_____

_____

_____

_____

_____

_____

Jesus Prays for Unity among Believers:

*What have you done to help foster greater unity among believers
regardless of their racial or cultural backgrounds?*

My prayer is not for them alone. I pray also for those who will believe in Me through their message, that all of them may be one, Father, just as you are in Me and I am in you. May they also be in you so that the world may believe that you have sent Me.

I have given them the glory that you gave Me, that they may be one as We are one: I in them and You in Me. May they be brought to complete unity to let the world know that You sent Me and have loved them even as You have loved Me.

Father, I want those You have given Me to be with Me where I am, and to see My glory, the glory You have given me because You loved me before the creation of the world.

Righteous Father, though the world does not know You, I know You, and they know that You have sent Me. I have made You known in order that the love You have for Me may be in them and that I myself may be in them.

John 17:20-26

Observations

Jesus Christ, before being arrested, prays for Himself, then prays for His disciples, and finally, He prays for believers. Jesus desires for believers to walk in a spirit of unity. He desires for all believers to have a close relationship with Him. Jesus wants the relationship between Him and believers to be similar to the intimate relationship that He has with the Father. Jesus wants believers to walk together in such a spirit of unity that the world may believe that He was sent by the Father.

The devil wants the Church to be divided. When the world sees a divided Church, they fail to see a risen Savior but instead they see people—who they refer to as hypocrites—getting together to have some meetings in a building. While the devil has a number of ways that he seeks to cause divisions, he tries to divide the Church over the issues regarding race and religion. Many churches and denominations have become divided and even split over these two issues. God's glory cannot be found at work among believers who have become divided over issues that take precedent over the Gospel being preached to a dying and hurting world.

The devil has used prejudice, bigotry, and racism as powerful spiritual weapons to cause division among believers. Many persons of color historically left churches that have mostly consisted of persons of non-color in the United States because they did not feel welcomed or celebrated. This is one of the major reasons why churches across America tend to consist of people that come from the same racial background. The racial composition of churches will not change until pastors, church leaders, laity, and denominational leaders become serious about dealing with their hearts regarding the issues of prejudice, bigotry, and racism.

John in the following Bible Scripture verses talks about the importance of loving your brother: "Dear friends, let us love one another, for love comes from God. Everyone who loves has been born of God and knows God. Whoever does not love does not know God, because God is love" (1 John 4:7-8).

"This is how we know what love is: Jesus Christ laid down his life for us. And we ought to lay down our lives for our brothers. If anyone has material possessions and sees his brother in need but has not pity on him, how can the love of God be in him?" (1 John 3:16-17).

"Dear friends, since God so loved us, we also ought to love one another. No one has ever seen God; but if we love one another, God lives in us and his love is made complete in us" (1 John 4:11-12).

"We love because he first loved us. If anyone says, 'I love God,' yet hates his brother, he is a liar. For anyone who does not love his brother, whom he has seen, cannot love God, whom he has not seen. And he has given us this command: Whoever loves God must also love his brother" (1 John 4:19-21).

"Anyone who hates his brother is a murderer, and you know that no murderer has eternal life in him" (1 John 3:15).

Please take a few moments to examine your own heart concerning prejudice, bigotry, and racism. Do you need to repent of any sin in your heart and ask God to forgive you?

Personal Reflections

- Please take a few moments and write down your initial reactions or thoughts concerning the scriptural passage._____

  _____

  _____

  _____

  _____

  _____

  _____

  _____

  _____

- Please take a few moments and write down what further insight you were able to gain from the scriptural passage as a result of reading the author's observation._____

  _____

  _____

  _____

  _____

  _____

  _____

  _____

  _____

- How do you intend to take the scriptural passage and what further information you obtained from reading the commentary and apply it to your life? _____

  _____

  _____

  _____

  _____

  _____

  _____

  _____

  _____

The Tower of Babel:

Did you know that we will not be very successful achieving racial diversity and unity in our churches if we attempt to obtain it our way rather than God's way?

Now the whole world had one language and a common speech. As men moved eastward, they found a plain in Shinar and settled there.

They said to each other, "Come, let's make bricks and bake them thoroughly." They used brick instead of stone, and tar for mortar. Then they said, "Come, let us build ourselves a city, with a tower that reaches to the heavens, so that we may make a name for ourselves and not be scattered over the face of the whole earth."

But the Lord came down to see the city and the tower that the men were building. The Lord said, "If as one people speaking the same language they have begun to do this, then nothing they plan to do will be impossible for them. Come, let us go down and confuse their language so they will not understand each other."

So the Lord scattered them from there over all the earth, and they stopped building the city. That is why it was called Babel—because there the Lord confused the language of the whole world. From there the Lord scattered them over the face of the whole earth.

Genesis 11:1-8

Observations

Many people over the years have falsely believed that God confused the languages and scattered the Shinarite people in Genesis 11 because He wanted the races to be separated. This false assumption could be no further from the truth. Many hate groups in the United States have bought into this lie and have used this as justification to support their belief that the races should be separated. God's judgment fell upon the Shinarite people because they became prideful and got outside of God's will for their lives. The pride and arrogance of the Shinarite people were clearly documented by, Number one, their desire to build the city of Babylon with a tower that would reach heaven. Number two: They desired to make a name for themselves. Number three was their desire to not be scattered over the earth. By sinning against God, the Shinarite people invited God's judgment to come into their lives.

God chose to judge the Shinarite people by confusing their language and scattering them throughout the earth. Whenever believers allow pride to cause them to exalt themselves, attempt to make a name for themselves, and rebel against God's will, then they invite the judgment of God to come into their lives. The Shinarite people were so prideful that they actually believed that they could build the city of Babylon with a tower that reached to heaven. They simply wanted to make a name for themselves and somehow prevent God from scattering them throughout the earth.

This ran contrary to the following instructions that God gave Adam and Eve in Genesis 1:28: "God blessed them and said to them, 'Be fruitful and increase in number; fill the earth and subdue it. Rule over the fish of the sea and the birds of the air and every living creature that moves on the ground.'"

The Shinarite people's desire to not be scattered over the earth also ran contrary to the following instruction that God gave Noah in Genesis 9:7: "As for you, be fruitful and increase in number; multiplying on earth and increase upon it."

The Shinarite people were seeking to glorify themselves based upon their words and their actions. They wanted to build a tower to heaven so they could say, "Look what we have accomplished!" These people foolishly believed that they could prevent God from scattering them throughout the earth. They were deceived into thinking that by their own strength they could walk in unity as a people—without God. We desperately need God if we are going to walk in unity within the Church and among fellow believers.

The following lessons can be learned from the story about the Tower of Babel that are applicable to the Church today:

1. We will never obtain racial diversity and unity in our churches until such efforts are completely born out of prayer rather than human strength.
2. We will never obtain racial diversity and unity in our churches as long as pride and arrogance are rampant.
3. We will never be able to obtain racial diversity and unity in our churches as long as we stick to our own agenda rather than God's agenda.
4. We will never obtain racial diversity and unity in our churches as long as we refuse to develop cross-cultural friendships and relationships with one another.
5. We will never be able to obtain racial diversity and unity in our churches until we allow God to change our hearts.
6. We will never be able to obtain racial diversity and unity in our churches if we try to take the credit or receive the glory for what God is doing or has done in the past.
7. We will never be able to obtain racial diversity or unity in our churches if our words or actions are not genuine.
8. We will never be able to obtain racial diversity and unity in our churches if we attempt to do things that are contrary to God's will.
9. We will never be able to obtain racial diversity and unity in our churches until believers are ready to throw pride out the window and replace it with humility.

God judged the Shinarite people for their sin and rebellion. He confused their language so they would not understand one another and scattered them throughout the earth. All the work on the tower came to a screeching halt because the people could no longer understand one another. They were not able to achieve what they had originally set out to accomplish. We can never achieve anything that is contrary to God's will.

They sought to accomplish their own agenda rather than God's agenda. Who could imagine what the Shinarite people would have set out to accomplish next had God not put a stop to their rebellion? Perhaps they would have thought that they could "overthrow" God if they would have succeeded in building their tower that would supposedly reach to the heavens.

Many pastors of non-color across the United States have wanted to reach out to persons of color and embrace racial diversity, but either they did not know what to do or they simply went about trying to obtain it the wrong way. Whenever we replace God's agenda with our own agenda, we have set ourselves up to fail miserably at whatever task we undertake.

It is almost embarrassing and shameful to admit but the secular world has done more to address prejudice, bigotry and racism than the Church. This is a disgrace, because the Church is the only institution that has the real answer to the racial problems that plagues America and the rest of the world. The Church's solution to the problem can only be found in Jesus Christ. Only the Gospel of Jesus Christ can help believers break through the racial barriers that the devil has erected to try and stop people from all races from coming together to worship God within our churches.

We need to make sure that we discern God's heart for racial and cultural diversity within our churches. Pastors of non-color and their church members have invited persons of color to visit on Sunday morning, however, once the people arrived at their doorsteps, they did not feel welcomed or celebrated. When people from diverse racial and cultural backgrounds attend a church for the first time, they know whether or not they are being celebrated or simply tolerated. When we tolerate people, we put up with them even though we would rather not have them around. However, when we choose to celebrate people, this means that we really love them, accept them without any strings being attached, completely value how God has gifted them, and how much our lives would be incomplete without them.

Churches must continually look for ways to share the Gospel in such a way that everyone feels welcome and are able to participate despite language barriers. Language translators and translation audio equipment can play a very important role in helping to address the needs of people who do not speak English as a primary or secondary language. As the

United States becomes more racially diverse and the number of immigrants continues to increase, then pastors and their churches will be challenged to do even more to help breakdown any language barriers that may prevent some people from coming to church. Has your church taken the necessary steps to address any potential language barriers?

Prayer is absolutely essential in helping to develop a vision for how your church can reach out to persons of other racial backgrounds. Do people from diverse racial and cultural backgrounds that visit your church feel welcome when they attend? Do you celebrate or simply tolerate the persons of color that visit or become members of your church?

Personal Reflections

■ Please take a few moments and write down your initial reactions or thoughts concerning the scriptural passage._____

_____

_____

_____

_____

_____

_____

_____

■ Please take a few moments and write down what further insight you were able to gain from the scriptural passage as a result of reading the author's observation._____

_____

_____

_____

_____

_____

_____

_____

■ How do you intend to take the scriptural passage and what further information you obtained from reading the commentary and apply it to your life?_____

_____

_____

_____

_____

_____

_____

_____

Paul Admonishes Believers to Avoid Divisions in the Church:

Have you helped encourage unity or division within your local church?

I appeal to you, brothers, in the name of our Lord Jesus Christ, that all of you agree with one another so that there may be no divisions among you and that you may be perfectly united in mind and thought. My brothers, some from Chloe's household have informed me that there are quarrels among you. What I mean is this: One of you says, "I follow Paul;" another, "I follow Apollos;" another, "I follow Cephas;" still another, "I follow Christ."

Is Christ divided? Was Paul crucified for you? Were you baptized into the name of Paul? I am thankful that I did not baptize any of you except Crispus and Gaius, so no one can say that you were baptized into my name. (Yes, I also baptized the household of Stephanas; beyond that, I don't remember if I baptized anyone else.) For Christ did not send me to baptize, but to preach the Gospel—not with words of human wisdom, lest the cross of Christ be emptied of its power.

1 Corinthians 1:10-17

Observations

Paul urged his fellow believers in the local church to walk in agreement with one another in an effort to avoid divisions. The devil looks for any way that he can sow seeds of division into the hearts of believers. We must guard our hearts and minds when it comes to dealing with issues that are debatable and divisive within the local church. As believers, we should be careful to avoid engaging in gossip and slander about other church members.

Paul did not want any seeds of division to be found among believers within the Corinthian church. Many churches have become divided—and even split—over issues regarding pastoral transition, personnel changes, financial management, facilities management, leadership issues, the church vision, conflict between church members, church scandals, church board conflicts, racial diversity and even the color of the carpet.

Paul did not want any quarrels to be found among church members in the local church. He knew that a lot of discussions and healthy debate would take place within the church, but once all the talking had ceased at the table and a decision had been made, then no disagreement should be found between church members. We can cause division within the church when we allow pride to cause us to go to great extremes to win an argument or to prove that we are right rather than asking ourselves the following question: What would Jesus do? We need to walk in humility and be led by the power of the Holy Spirit if we are going to have racial unity within the church.

Provided below is a list of potential barriers that make it very difficult to obtain racial diversity within the Church:

- Pastor and leadership team refuses to provide the necessary leadership on issues concerning racial diversity and inclusiveness.
- Pastor and leadership team refuses to address incidents that occur within the church that would be considered to be racially insensitive.
- Church members make inappropriate comments or jokes within the church that would be offensive to persons of color.
- Pastor and leadership team refuses to promptly address any racially-motivated incidents that take place within the church.

- Church members become resistant to the whole idea of having racial diversity within their church.
- Church members deny that prejudice, bigotry and racism are problems that need to be addressed.
- Church members refuse to change their own hearts regarding the issues of prejudice, bigotry, and racism.
- Church members become resistant to changes that need to be made within their church so it can become racially inclusive.
- Church members refuse to develop cross-cultural relationships with one another.
- Church members become offended due to changes being made to reach out to persons of color and begin to leave church in rather large numbers.

The Church can be the best training ground for believers to practice walking in racial unity with one another, because there will be no prejudice, bigotry, or racism that can be found in heaven. God only needs believers that are willing to reach out as ambassadors to people in love with the Gospel regardless of their racial and cultural background.

John said the following in Revelation 7:9: "After this I looked and there before me was a great multitude that no one could count, from every nation, tribe, people and language, standing before the throne and in front of the Lamb."

God could have chosen to have a great multitude of believers stand before His throne one day that would all come from same race. However, God's Word reveals that the great multitude of people that will stand before His throne will consist of people who come from diverse racial and cultural backgrounds.

Have you helped create unity or division within your local church? When it comes to the issue of racial diversity have you worked hard to bring people from diverse racial and cultural backgrounds within your church together or helped create division based upon your words and actions? We can only have racial diversity in our churches if we choose to walk in the footsteps of Jesus Christ. We must be led by the Holy Spirit in what we say and what we do.

Personal Reflections

■ Please take a few moments and write down your initial reactions or thoughts concerning the scriptural passage._____

_____

_____

_____

_____

_____

_____

_____

■ Please take a few moments and write down what further insight you were able to gain from the scriptural passage as a result of reading the author's observation._____

_____

_____

_____

_____

_____

_____

_____

■ How do you intend to take the scriptural passage and what further information you obtained from reading the commentary and apply it to your life?_____

_____

_____

_____

_____

_____

_____

The So-Called Curse of Ham:

Do you belong to any organization or work for a company
that practices institutional racism? Are you a racist?

The sons of Noah who came out of the ark were Shem, Ham, and Japheth. (Ham was the father of Canaan.) These were the three sons of Noah, and from them came the people who were scattered over the earth. Noah, a man of the soil, proceeded to plant a vineyard. When he drank some of its wine, he became drunk and lay uncovered inside his tent. Ham, the father of Canaan, saw his father's nakedness and told his two brothers outside. But Shem and Japheth took a garment and laid it across their shoulders; then they walked in backward and covered their father's nakedness. Their faces were turned the other way so that they would not see their father's nakedness.

When Noah awoke from his wine and found out what his youngest son had done to him, he said, "Cursed be Canaan! The lowest of slaves will he be to his brothers."

He also said, "Blessed be the Lord, the God of Shem! May Canaan be the slave of Shem. May God extend the territory of Japheth; may Japheth live in the tents of Shem, and may Canaan be his slave."

Genesis 9:18-27

Observations

The above scriptural passage has often been misunderstood and misinterpreted by many people. This biblical story begins by identifying the sons of Noah that came out of the ark. The sons of Noah included Shem, Ham, and Japheth. The descendants that came from Noah's sons were eventually scattered all over the earth. Noah planted a vineyard but apparently became drunk and never completed the task that he had set out to accomplish. As a result of Noah being intoxicated after drinking wine, he laid down and went to sleep in the tent without covering himself. Apparently Ham walked into the tent and saw his father laying down without any clothes on, and rather than covering his father up, he chose to leave him the way he found him and inform his two brothers about the problem that were outside the tent. However, Shem and Japheth chose to act responsibly; they walked into the tent backwards, so they would not be able to look upon their father's nakedness, and covered him up. When Noah woke up, he cursed Canaan and his descendants.

Some people have falsely believed that Noah cursed Ham and that as a result, African people should be enslaved. Noah would have had to curse Ham and his descendants or Ham's son Cush and his descendants for such a belief to have been proven to be credible. However, no curse was ever placed on Ham and his descendants or Cush and his descendants. The recipient of the curse was Canaan, the son of Ham, and his descendants. There were also those who falsely believed that Africans were descendants of Canaan. As a result, they tried to advance a flawed theory that people of African descent were cursed; their skin was dark as a result of being cursed, and they should be enslaved. This theory was even advanced to try and legitimize the practice of slavery. African people were not descendants of Canaan, as some people were falsely led to believe. They were actually descendants of Ham's son Cush. His descendants settled in Africa, and Canaan's descendants settled in Palestine.

Many people and institutions that were actively engaged in enslaving African people, believed that they were cursed, based upon their misinterpretation of the Scripture. African people were subjected to slavery as early as the fifteenth century. The actual practice did not get under way in the United States until 1619. It is estimated that as many as 10 million African people were brought to America on slave ships. African people were taken against their will from their homes and separated from their families to become slaves in America. African slaves had to endure the one-way trip to America on ships that is referred to as the Middle Passage. The slaves were chained together on these ships according to twos by their hands and feet. The slave traders that were motivated by financial greed chose to overload their ships with African slaves so they could reap much larger profits. Some scholars believe that it took on the average six to sixteen weeks for slaves to actually reach America from Africa by ship.[15] As a result of overcrowding conditions on the slave ships many diseases such as small- pox, dysentery and influenza swept through the ships. The mortality rates on the ships were believed to be between 25 and 40 percent during the early years of the slave trade according to some scholars.[16]

Many churches were divided over the issue of slavery at the end of the Civil War, based upon whether they were located in the North or the South. There were pastors who, through their own misinterpretation of Scripture, felt that based upon Genesis 9:13-27 slavery was sanctioned by God. However, not all Christians agreed with them. There were some Christians that belonged to the Abolitionist movement that felt slavery was an immoral practice that should be abolished. They strongly advocated against slave labor in Europe, America, and Africa. Slave owners very vigorously resisted the views and actions of those who belonged to the Abolitionist movement. They were concerned that their economic base would collapse if slavery ended and that they would no longer be able to meet the labor demands on the large plantations.

Racism has been defined as prejudice plus power. It can be practiced at the *individual level* and at the *institutional level*. Slavery was perpetuated in America for over 246 years because many racist individuals and the institutions they belonged to were willing to make sure that this immoral system continued to thrive economically. Slave traders, plantation owners, corporate leaders, politicians, judges, religious leaders, law enforcement officials, and others engaged in racist behavior at the individual level to ensure that slavery as a system was able to survive. These leaders collectively used their prejudice plus their power at the institutional level to subjugate and enslave African people. Racism can be very devastating and harmful to its victims. There are many people that still need healing in their lives as a result of being negatively impacted by racism. We have seen how racism has reared its ugly head during the Holocaust that led to the extermination of 5.6-5.9 million Jews by order of Adolf Hitler, the leader of the Nazi Party in Germany from 1939 till 1945.

This has been further evidenced by the policy of apartheid being introduced in South Africa during the 1940s to racially segregate the white minority from the non-white majority of the population (this unjust policy was abolished by President F.W. De Klerk in 1990, which led to the eventual release of Nelson Mandela from prison); ethnic cleansing being introduced by Slobodan Milosevic in Sarajevo, Bosnia's capital and Kosovo in an effort to eliminate the non-Serb population during the 1990s; and the expulsion of Native Americans from land that belonged to them in the United States, the slaughter of their people and racist policies that were enacted by the federal government that have had a negative impact on Native American people.

Have you ever spoken words or engaged in any behavior that would be considered to be racist? Do you need to seek God's forgiveness and repent for making any verbal comments or for taking any actions that would be considered to be racist?

Do you belong to any organization or work for a company that either currently or has in the past engaged in institutional racism? Do you need to seek God's forgiveness for being a part of an organization or company that has engaged in institutional racism? How can you become a change agent and effectively begin to address racism at the institutional level?

Personal Reflections

■ Please take a few moments and write down your initial reactions or thoughts concerning the scriptural passage._____

_____

_____

_____

_____

_____

_____

_____

■ Please take a few moments and write down what further insight you were able to gain from the scriptural passage as a result of reading the author's observation._____

_____

_____

_____

_____

_____

_____

_____

■ How do you intend to take the scriptural passage and what further information you obtained from reading the commentary and apply it to your life?_____

_____

_____

_____

_____

_____

_____

_____

_____

A lot of people remark how the situation of the Church in the twenty-first Century is similar to the Church in the first Century, and there is much to ponder in this regard. However, there is one significant difference. In the first Century, to most of the world, Christianity was an unknown religion. In the twenty-first Century, to much of the world, it is a failed religion—and foremost among our failures is our failure to bring greater reconciliation among races. One wonders how the world would be different if even fifty percent of the energy invested in ecclesiastical argument over the last five hundred years had instead been invested in fighting racism and demonstrating reconciliation, with followers of Jesus loving their neighbors whatever their race, religion, or ethnic background. May we invest our lives in that pursuit in the years ahead!

- Brian D. McLaren, Pastor and Best-Selling author, *A New Kind of Christian*

Racism has been around for over two hundred years, and because of that longevity and because of the pronounced separation of the races in this nation, it can be said that racism is institutionalized within our society. That means that racism is entrenched within our government, corporations, and, last but certainly not least, the Church. The mere silence by some of these institutions constitutes approval, and I find the pronounced silence of the Church most disturbing.

- Bob Woodrick, Chairman & C.E.O. of D & W Food Centers, Inc.

Racism is either thinking or saying to a person that, "I know you need me, I will try to help you but I really don't need you."

- Coach Bill McCartney, President/Founder of Promise Keepers

WWJD -He would find the most disenfranchised, hurting person and take a straight path through their life.

WWJD -He would not politely smile while thinking thoughts that were bigoted, prejudice, and racist.

WWJD -He would so minister dignity that it would lift people and tell them, "It does not matter what history says, it's all about the future; it's about the breakthrough; it's about the incredible new thing that God wants to do in your life!"

- Scott Hagan, Senior Pastor and author of *They Walked with the Savior*

The depth of racism in the structural, cultural and psychic history of the United States has seldom been fully comprehended. Perhaps we have yet to get to the heart of the problem because we have failed to perceive the fundamental spiritual and theological roots of racism in America. The idol of "whiteness" and the assumptions of white privilege and supremacy have yet to be spiritually confronted in America, and even in churches. There is more to do than educating, organizing, advocating, changing consciousness, and changing policies. In addition to the hard work of personal relationships, community building, and political and economic change, other responses may be required—like confession, prayer, conversion, and forgiveness.

- Jim Wallis, Editor in Chief and author for *Sojourners Magazine*

Racism and oppression are from the very pit of hell. Now is the time for us to stand up and speak out, to put a stop to the undercurrent of racism that we so politely tolerate. Only the church can strike the lethal blow at the very roots of racism and oppression, hatred and bigotry. Only the church, through its teaching and yielding to the work of the Holy Spirit, can change the minds and attitudes of people.

- Dr. Jefferson D. Edwards, Jr., Pastor and author of *Purging Racism from Christianity*

Racism and segregation in the church will quickly collapse when Christians and local churches begin to initiate fellowship with believers from other races, cultures, and nations. The pernicious viruses that cause racism—fear, ignorance, and racial superiority complexes—cannot survive in such a radiant and tranquil setting.

- Michael E. Goings, Pastor and author of *Free At Last?*

FIVE

SUGGESTIONS FOR
PASTORS OF NON-COLOR

1. Examine your own heart when it comes to dealing with the issues of prejudice, bigotry, and racism.
2. Provide biblically-based cultural sensitivity training for the church.
3. Publicly condemn prejudice, bigotry, and racism from the pulpit.
4. Teach a biblically-based series on prejudice, bigotry, and racism.
5. Challenge the entire church to examine their own hearts when it comes to the issues of prejudice, bigotry, and racism.
6. Ask God to speak to you regarding what your leadership team and church congregation can do to address these issues.
7. Obtain support from the church leadership team to put together a strategic plan to foster greater racial and cultural unity within your church and the surrounding community. The strategic plan should be updated as needed.

8. Don't just hire people that look like you to work on your staff. Hire talented men and women to work on your staff that are representative of God's Kingdom. Also, don't hire a person of color to be a token or solely for appearance purposes.

9. Periodically invite pastors of color to preach at your church.

10. Develop good friendships and working relationships with pastors of color within your communities.

11. Develop church partnerships with churches in the urban community. And consider investing human and financial resources into these churches and their communities.

12. Examine your church's internal and external programming to ensure that they are not biased toward persons of color.

13. Advertise church services and special events in newspapers and on radio and television stations that reach persons of color.

14. Provide some supplier, vendor, construction and professional service opportunities to businesses that are owned by persons of color.

15. Encourage your church's music minister and/or choir director to explore culturally diverse styles of praise and worship. Strongly consider including songs written by persons of color in your church service.

16. Invite persons of color to lead conferences or speak at special events at your church.

17. Send missionaries to the urban community and not just overseas. Don't forget about the wonderful mission opportunities right in your own backyard.

18 Consider providing language translation services for people who may need interpretative services.

19. Conduct evangelism efforts in the urban community. Spend time spreading the Gospel in the urban community and don't just pick up speed when you drive through it.

20. Consider learning a foreign language and learning more about other countries.

21. Value racial and cultural diversity in your church congregation. Appreciate what you have in common and what you do not have in common with persons of color.

22. Don't expect a "one size fits all" church ministry to be very effective in reaching people from diverse racial and cultural backgrounds.

23. Be willing to change or make the necessary adjustments at your church in order to have racial diversity and unity.

Personal Reflections

Scripture Reference: 1 Samuel 16:7

■ Please take a few moments and write down how some of the suggestions may assist you in addressing bigotry, prejudice, and racism:

_____

_____

_____

_____

_____

_____

_____

_____

_____

■ How could you implement some of the suggestions?

_____

_____

_____

_____

_____

_____

_____

_____

■ What are some other things that come to mind that you could do to
address bigotry, prejudice, and racism?_____

_____

_____

_____

_____

_____

_____

Racism is not only a social problem.... Because racism is a sin, it is also a moral and spiritual issue. Legal and social efforts to obliterate racism (or at least curb its more onerous effects) have a legitimate place. However, only the supernatural love of God can change our hearts in a lasting way and replace hatred and indifference with love and active compassion.

- Reverend Billy Graham

Sometimes change comes not in the first round, but at the second, third, or fourth. Change starts with one person questioning, challenging, speaking up, and doing something to make a difference. We can make a difference because each of us is already part of a community where racism exists and strives. We are connected to neighborhoods, workplaces, schools, and religious organizations. Our connections, our relationships, or positions in these organizations give us some leverage to make a difference.

- Paul Kivel, Author of *Uprooting Racism*

Living a multi-cultural lifestyle is everyone's responsibility.

- Dr. David Ireland, Pastor and author of *What Color Is Your God?*

As a white woman, as long as I do not work against white Christian racism, I carry the guilt of ongoing racist speech, structures, and actions, both my own and others. I do not need to be actively racist myself in order to carry responsibility for racism. The structures in which I live and work will do that for me. I need only keep silent. Silence in the pulpit, in the classroom, in the office, at the bowling alley, at home. Silence. When white people do nothing to combat the racist assumptions and privileges with which we have been taught to function, we continue to foster the oppressive structures from which we unwittingly benefit. When we fail to act, we acquiesce in the corrosive and deadly sin, which subverts and denies God's creation and salvation of the world.

-Susan E. Davies, Professor and Author of *Ending Racism in the Church*

In Scripture, holy ground is where groups of those formerly estranged and separated become one, new, unlikely people under Christ. Yet America's Christians have come to accept as normal and acceptable the racial fragmentation of the body of Christ that is the church. The idea of "white churches" and "black churches," and the history of alienation, superiority, and exclusion that created them, does not disturb us. The question is not how will the church heal America's race problem. The question is: Are Christians willing by addressing our racial divide to learn to become the church?

- Chris Rice, Author of *More than Equals and Grace Matters*

We need to ask ourselves two other questions: "What have we lost as white people because of racism?" and "What have we to gain with the end of racism?" These questions become easier to answer as we become more aware of the extent to which racism imprisons us. For we have lost so very much, and we have so very much to gain. As each of us struggles with these questions, we need to look for change in our lives. If we are to have a lasting commitment to the struggle, we need also to know how we ourselves will benefit from a world without racism.

- Joseph Barndt, Author of *Dismantling Racism*

Somewhere along the line we're going to have to quit lying to our children or at least have enough courage to apologize for lying. We've told them God can do everything. We've told them God can raise the dead, open up blind eyes, we've even told them that God can heal AIDS. But He just can't deal with this racial problem. So now we either have to quit lying or live the truth and apologize. These kids are growing up mingling with everybody and then they're going to come to our churches and what are they going to see? They are going to be confused!

- Marilyn Burnett Abplanalp, Professor of Ethnic Inclusion in Pastoral Leadership in the Assemblies of God Fellowship from 1906-1999
(This quote was taken from a pastor whose name was not released in the dissertation.)

SIX

SUGGESTIONS FOR
PERSONS OF NON-COLOR

1. Examine your own heart when it comes to dealing with the issues of prejudice, bigotry, and racism.
2. Value what you have in common with people from different racial and cultural backgrounds.
3. Value what you do not have in common with people from different racial and cultural backgrounds.
4. Be willing to learn more about people from different racial and cultural groups.
5. Develop friendships with people from different racial and cultural groups. Don't just spend all your time with people who look, act or think like you.
6. Recognize that God has given all believers the ministry of reconciliation.
7. Invite persons of color to visit your church.
8. Don't allow fear to stop you from developing friendships with persons of color. Remember, God has not given you the spirit of fear.

9. Don't expect a person of color to necessarily think, act, talk, or express an opinion in the same manner as you.
10. Provide persons of color with an opportunity to share some of their experiences with prejudice, bigotry and racism.
11. Read books and articles written by or about persons of color.
12. Don't always assume your way of doing things is the best approach that should be taken. Persons of color may provide further insight or bring a fresh perspective to the board, committee or special project.
13. Develop an appreciation of different styles of worship.
14. Develop an appreciation for music written or sung by persons from different racial or cultural backgrounds.
15. Prayerfully consider doing some missionary work within the urban community.
16. Prayerfully consider doing some evangelism within the urban community.
17. Carefully listen to what persons of color have to say.
18. Value the advice or counsel that persons of color provide you with on a regular basis. Good communication is the key in establishing strong friendships with people from different racial or cultural backgrounds.
19. Consider learning a foreign language and learning more about other countries.
20. Encourage your children to develop friendships with people from different racial and cultural backgrounds.
21. Do not deny that prejudice, bigotry, and racism is not prevalent in the church and within your local community. Don't try to force persons of color to assimilate to your culture.
22. Do not resist necessary changes being made at your church in order to reach people from different racial and cultural backgrounds with the Gospel of Jesus Christ.
23. Be willing to change your way of thinking in some areas and adjust to doing some things differently at your church in order to welcome and celebrate people from diverse racial and cultural backgrounds.
24. Recognize that persons of color do not all look alike, think alike or act the same way.
25. Please make sure that you appreciate what makes each person of color's physical appearance, personality, gifts, and talents unique from other people you know.

Personal Reflections

Scripture Reference: Proverbs 27:19

■ Please take a few moments and write down how some of the suggestions may assist you in addressing bigotry, prejudice, and racism:

_____

_____

_____

_____

_____

_____

_____

_____

_____

■ How could you implement some of the suggestions?

_____

_____

_____

_____

_____

_____

_____

_____

■ What are some other things that come to mind that you could do to address bigotry, prejudice, and racism?_____

_____

_____

_____

_____

_____

_____

Racism is an irrational system that does not even benefit those who enforce it. On a personal level, it robs an individual of the ability to be fully human and to completely enjoy all the wonders that life has to offer. On a societal level racism deprives us of all of the talents that this nation needs to compete in our global economy. It creates two victims instead of one and traps them in a cycle of hatred. Such a system deeply deserves the death that we Christians must hasten to give it.

- Dr. George Yancey, Professor and author of *Beyond Black and White*

In the church, prejudice and bigotry are less blatant and more subtle. Much like the invisible and odorless carbon monoxide, the results can be fatal—but, they don't have to be! I have learned that racism is a matter of the heart, which may or may not be evidenced through actions. Therefore guard your heart against unforgiveness, bitterness, and retaliatory prejudice. At the end of the day, you are responsible for your actions and responses. That is what is meant by responsibility—respond ability! Don't place your emotional health in someone else's hands—stay healthy! Healthy people are conduits of healing. Be a healer.

- Dr. Samuel R. Chand, President of Beulah Heights Bible College

One of the Lord's most poignant parables deals with the issue of forgiveness. In the parable of the unforgiving servant (Matthew 18), our Heavenly Father represents the king and we His servants. The point of the parable is that each human being has an enormous debt he cannot pay. Each is a sinner, and the wages of sin is death. Jesus took our sin upon Himself and paid our debt to the Father. Our debt has been forgiven in full because of Jesus' sacrifice on the cross. We now have the glorious hope of spending eternity with God. This is the greatest gift any human being can receive. Jesus then asks us, "What exactly is it that you cannot forgive, since you have been forgiven so much?" Those who have been forgiven much, forgive much.

-Rachelle Hood-Phillips, Author of *Demolishing the Spiritual Stronghold of Racism in the American Church*

SEVEN

Suggestions for Pastors of Color

1. Establish friendships with pastors of non-color and pastors from different racial or cultural backgrounds.
2. Develop relationships with pastors of non-color and pastors from different racial or cultural backgrounds that are built based upon mutual respect and trust.
3. Develop partnerships with churches of non-color and churches of color.
4. Develop partnerships with pastors of non-color that do not require you to become a token or force you to assimilate to the dominant culture.
5. Seek God about developing a strategic plan for addressing prejudice, bigotry, and racism in your community.
6. Seek support and work collaboratively with pastors of non-color and pastors from different racial or cultural backgrounds in your community.
7. Consider inviting pastors of non-color and pastors from different racial or cultural backgrounds to preach at your church.
8. Forgive pastors of non-color and pastors of color that may have offended you in the past.

9. Support efforts by pastors of non-color, pastors of color or and other organizations to address racism, bigotry and prejudice within your community.

10. Share your life experiences in dealing with prejudice, bigotry, and racism with pastors of non-color.

11. Encourage your church members to forgive persons of non-color that have either spoken words or done things to them based upon prejudice, bigotry or racism.

12. Encourage your church members to also forgive persons of color that may have offended them in the past.

13. Do not allow efforts within the church to promote racial justice and unity to take precedence over God's Word being preached.

14. Do not allow the presence of your race or culture in the Bible to give you a feeling of superiority over other races.

15. Please do not allow anything to disturb the unity among believers within your church and local community.

16. Develop evangelism programs that far surpass reaching people from your own race.

17. Encourage your church to welcome persons of non-color and people from different racial and cultural backgrounds.

18. Build strong working relationships with pastors of non-color and pastors from different racial or cultural backgrounds that are not built upon suspicion, distrust or fear.

19. Periodically invite persons of non-color and persons from different racial or cultural backgrounds to speak at conferences or participate in special events at your church.

20. Encourage your church staff to develop cross-cultural friendships/relationships with persons of non-color and people from different racial and cultural backgrounds.

Personal Reflections

Scripture Reference: Matthew 6:21

■ Please take a few moments and write down how some of the suggestions may assist you in addressing bigotry, prejudice, and racism:

_____

_____

_____

_____

_____

_____

_____

■ How could you implement some of the suggestions?

_____

_____

_____

_____

_____

_____

_____

■ What are some other things that come to mind that you could do to address bigotry, prejudice, and racism?_____

_____

_____

_____

_____

_____

_____

The stronghold of racism isn't a human problem; it is a human symptom of a spiritual problem. We need to tear down the stronghold that has successfully invaded and wrecked human lives and divided the Church for centuries. All of us who call upon the name of Jesus, regardless of our color, nationality, or gender, need to declare and claim our freedom in Christ so we can offer it to others without shame or apology.

-Bishop Joseph L. Garlington, Pastor and author of *Right or Reconciled?*

While the storm of racism continues to batter our bodies and minds, its raging winds, its forceful waves, and its rising waters will never put out the fires of unity, determination and hope. Because that which stands before the storm is what we call the human spirit—a collective power that draws its strength from those who have come before and those who stand today. It's a spirit that no storm, not even racism, has overcome [or] will ever overcome.

- Dr. Steve L. Robbins, Director of the Woodrick Institute for the Study of Racism and Diversity

Culpability for the racist structures that still predominate in the country belongs to churches as well as governments and other institutions of society. Churches and Christians must challenge the structures of racism in society. If we accept the world as it is, we give in to a malaise that eats away at the souls of our people and other churches. This is a serious theological, social, political and spiritual problem that is going to take a generation to correct.

- Dr. George (Tink) Tinker, Professor and author, Iliff School of Theology

═══ Eight ═══

Suggestions for
Persons of Color

1. Develop friendships with persons of non-color and persons from different racial or cultural backgrounds.
2. Share your personal experiences with persons of non-color and with persons from different racial or cultural backgrounds.
3. Recognize that good communication skills are essential in developing good relationships with persons of non-color and persons from different racial or cultural backgrounds.
4. Support efforts of persons of non-color to address prejudice, bigotry, and racism in your community.
5. Periodically invite persons of non-color and persons from different racial or cultural backgrounds to attend your church.
6. Make sure that you forgive persons of non-color and persons from different racial or cultural backgrounds that may have offended you in the past.
7. Don't approach an opportunity to develop a friendship with a person of non-color with suspicion, distrust or fear.
8. Pray for people that have prejudice, bigotry, or racism in their hearts.

9. Teach your children to love people regardless of their racial or cultural background.

10. Recognize that developing a friendship with a person of non-color should not require you to lose your racial or cultural identity.

11. Appreciate what you have in common with persons of non-color and what you do not have in common with them.

12. Risk being offended, getting rejected, and possibly being misunderstood in your efforts to develop relationships with persons of non-color and persons from different racial and cultural backgrounds.

13. Make sure you open up, be honest, and share how you feel with persons of non-color and persons from different racial and cultural backgrounds. This is critical in establishing good friendships and relationships with one another.

14. Develop strong friendships and relationships with persons of non-color and persons from different racial and cultural backgrounds that are based upon perseverance.

15. Consider learning a foreign language.

16. Pray about doing missionary work within your community or overseas.

17. Determine what you can do to help promote racial unity and address issues concerning racial justice within your church and local community.

18. Provide your children with the opportunity to do some missionary work within your community or overseas.

19. Share your experiences with prejudice, bigotry, and racism with your children. Inform them about what God has taught you based upon your own life experiences.

20. Encourage your children to develop friendships with children of non-color and children from different racial and cultural backgrounds.

Personal Reflections

Scripture Reference: Psalm 16:7-8

■ Please take a few moments and write down how some of the suggestions may assist you in addressing bigotry, prejudice, and racism:

_____

_____

_____

_____

_____

_____

_____

_____

_____

■ How could you implement some of the suggestions? _____

_____

_____

_____

_____

_____

_____

_____

_____

■ What are some other things that come to mind that you could do to
address bigotry, prejudice, and racism? _____

_____

_____

_____

_____

_____

_____

NINE

DO YOU KNOW GOD?

Do you have any prejudice, bigotry, or racism in your heart? Have you ever treated someone differently because of the color of her skin? Have you ever had any prejudice, bigotry or racism perpetuated against you? Have you pursued the opportunity to heal as a result of being wounded from such an experience? Have you ever done anything to address bigotry, prejudice or racism? Would you like to find the real answer to the racial problems that plague this country or obtain healing for wounds that you have received as a result of being subjected to racial hatred? Would you like to know God?

Purpose, meaning, and a reason for living—these are all things we desire and search for in life. Despite steps each one of us takes to find purpose and meaning in life, we still fill empty and unfulfilled. That is because there is spiritual emptiness in each of our lives. We each have a hole in our hearts, a spiritual vacuum deep within our souls. Possessions won't fill this hole, nor will success. Relationships alone cannot satisfy this emptiness, and morality, in and of itself, falls miserably short of occupying this space. In fact, even religion cannot fill the void in our hearts (See John 4:13-15, 5:39-40; 6:63-65.).

God understood our problem and knew that we could not do anything about it. Because God loves us, He sent His own Son, Jesus Christ, to earth to bridge the chasm of sin that separates us from Him (see John 3:1-16; 6:47; 8:24). To know Jesus Christ personally and have your sins forgiven, you must believe that you are a sinner separated from God and that your only hope is Jesus Christ, the Son of God, who came and died for your sins. To stop here, however, would be to stop short of salvation. There are two things you must do to enter into a relationship with God, from whom you have been separated.

You must first turn from your sins. As Jesus began His public ministry, His message was, "Turn from your sins" (Mark 1:15). He was telling the people to repent—to acknowledge their sins, change their minds, and change the direction of their lives.

Look at it this way. In the past, we have been blinded by our sin, causing us to run from God. As we repent, we do a U-turn and start running toward Him. It is not enough just to be sorry for our sins. We must also change our lifestyle, for the Bible teaches that "God can use sorrow in our lives to help us turn away from sin and seek salvation" (2 Corinthians 7:10). In other words, if you are really sorry for something, it will result in a change in your actions.

The apostle Paul summed up this change succinctly when he quoted Jesus, who said that people must turn "from the darkness to light, and from the power of Satan to God, so that they will receive forgiveness of sins and a place among those who are sanctified by faith in Me" (Acts 26:18). You see, there are some things only God can do and some things only you can do. Only God can remove your sins and give you the gift of eternal life, but only you can turn from your sins and receive Jesus as your Savior. That brings up the second thing you must do to respond to God's offer.

You must believe in and receive Jesus Christ into your life. Having seen the enormity of your sin and having decided to turn away from it, you then must believe in and receive Jesus Christ as your Lord and Savior. Becoming a Christian, however, is far more than following a creed or trying to live by certain standards. Jesus said that you must be "born again," or more literally, "born from above" (John 3:3). This spiritual rebirth happens when we personally believe in Jesus Christ, receive Him by inviting Him into our lives, and turn from our sins. In other words, we ask Jesus to come and take residence in our lives, making the changes He deems necessary. A person must take this all-important step in order to become a child of God.

Notice that this offer is yours for the asking, and it is free. You don't have to work for it, trying to clean up your life before you make this life-changing decision. The Bible says, "The free gift of God is eternal life through Christ Jesus our Lord" (Romans 6:23).

Being a Christian also means having a relationship with the living God. In Revelation 3:20, Jesus said, "Here I am! I stand at the door and knock. If anyone hears My voice and opens the door, I will come in and eat with him, and he with Me." To better understand the meaning of this verse, it is important to understand the culture at the time it was written. Eating together in Bible times was a long, drawn out affair. People would not sit on chairs behind tables in a formal setting as we do, but they would often sit on the ground, reclining on pillows around a low table. The relaxed atmosphere made meals a time when you would not only satisfy your appetite but also receive a gratifying serving of enjoyable table conversation. You would share your heart and life with those who sat beside you.

Consequently, when Jesus says that He will share a meal with us, it implies intimacy, closeness, and friendship. He offers this to us, but we must first hear him calling us. To hear God calling us, we must know how He speaks. One way in which God speaks to us is described on occasion as a still, small voice. This could be described in another way: as that tug you may have felt on your heart from the Holy Spirit showing you your need for Jesus. He may even be speaking to you right now! It is at that point that you must open the door. Only you can do that; Jesus will not force His way in. Did you know that God will even forgive you for having any prejudice, bigotry, or racism in your heart?

RECEIVING JESUS CHRIST INTO YOUR HEART

If you are ready to turn from your sins and believe in Jesus Christ so that you can receive forgiveness and the hope of eternal life, then take a moment to bow your head and pray a prayer like this one:

God, I'm sorry for my sin. I turn from it right now. I thank you for sending Jesus Christ to die on the cross for my sin. Jesus, I ask you to come into my heart and life right now. Be my Lord, Savior, and friend. Help me to follow You all the days of my life as your disciple. Thank you for forgiving and receiving me right now. Thank you that my sin is forgiven and that I am going to heaven.

In Jesus' name I pray, Amen.

REDEDICATING YOUR LIFE TO JESUS CHRIST

Perhaps you are already a Christian but you have strayed from Jesus Christ. You have been a prodigal son or daughter. God will forgive you right now if you will return to Him. He tells us in Scripture, "My way-ward children," says the Lord, "come back to Me, and I will heal your way-ward hearts" (Jeremiah 3:22) [New Living].

If you would like to return to God and rededicate your life to Him right now, you may want to pray something like this:

God, I am sorry for my sin. I am sorry that I have strayed from You. I ask you to forgive me now as I repent of my sin. I don't want to live like a prodigal any longer. Renew and revive me as I once again follow you as my God. Thank you for your forgiveness.
In Jesus' name I pray, Amen.

Whether you prayed to make a first-time commitment or a recommitment, you have made the right decision. God has forgiven and received it if you really meant it. If you have harbored any prejudice, bigotry, or racism in your heart, it has been washed away. Know that your relationship with Jesus Christ will bring radical and dramatic changes in your life. Describing this, the Bible says, "What this means is that those who become Christians become new persons. They are not the same anymore, for the old life is gone. A new life has begun!" (2 Corinthians 5:17) [New Living]. Now that is good news! But more importantly, God has changed your eternal destiny. Instead of fearing eternal punishment in a place called hell, you will spend peaceful eternity in His presence in heaven.

WHAT YOU SHOULD DO NOW THAT YOU'VE ACCEPTED JESUS CHRIST OR REDEDICATED YOUR LIFE TO HIM

1. Find a good church to attend and become a member so you can grow spiritually.
2. Develop a strong prayer life.
3. Begin reading your Bible on a daily basis.
4. Attend a bible study at your church, and learn more about God's Word.
5. Determine what spiritual gift(s) God has given you to use.
6. Get involved at your local church.
7. Recognize that you now belong to a Christian community. You can now enjoy their fellowship of believers that make up this wonderful community.

Special Note: All paragraphs in the section entitled "Do You Know God?", with exception of the first paragraph, were drafted by Evangelist Greg Laurie of Harvest Crusades. Special permission has been granted for these paragraphs regarding salvation and rededication to be included in this book. All rights reserved. The author has inserted any references to the terms prejudice, bigotry, and racism that appear in some of the paragraphs.

CONCLUSION

I pray that this book has affected your life. The sin of prejudice, bigotry, and racism needs to be purged from the heart of man. These sins have resulted in persons of color being denied opportunities to contribute their gifts and talents to the well-being of the nation. As a result, our country has experienced racial tensions and conflict because of its sin. America is in the process of becoming a much more racially diverse nation. Whether or not we truly learn to value racial and cultural diversity will have very important implications for all of us.

Demographic trends for the U.S. population based upon race and ethnicity indicate the following:

- The white population is shrinking. Whites will make up 72 percent of the U.S. population; 64 percent in 2020 and 53 percent by 2050.[17]
- The white population is getting older. By the year 2030 three fourths of the U.S. population will consist of whites 65 and older·[18]
- Between 2030 and 2050, the white population will be at zero population growth.[19]
- The racial and ethnic groups that will experience the largest growth will be the Hispanic-origin and Asian and Pacific Islander populations in the U.S.[20]
- The black population is expected to grow at nearly twice the rate than the white population.
- The white population will be the slowest-growing racial group.[21]
- Immigration will be a significant factor contributing to the growth among the Hispanic and Asian and Pacific Islander populations in the U.S.[22]
- According to the 2000 Census, the Hispanic population has become the largest minority group in the U.S.[23]

- The U.S. population will be very diverse in terms of race and ethnicity by the year 2050. Blacks will comprise 15 percent of the U.S. population; American Indian, Eskimo and Aleut 1 percent; Asian and Pacific Islanders 9 percent; Hispanic-origin population 25 percent and the white population will decline to 53 percent.[24]

What implications will the above population projections have on the United States? Based upon these projections, the following assumptions can be made:

- Americans need to deal with the issue of race before changes in the U.S. population lead to racial tension and conflict that could rival what this country has previously experienced.
- It will no longer be in the best interests of persons of non-color to ignore or simply deny that prejudice, bigotry, and racism does not exist without paying a very serious price.
- Because the U.S. population is in the process of becoming much more racially diverse, parents need to teach their children at a very early age to value racial diversity in order to lessen the potential for racial problems within our nation's schools.
- Embracing diversity in the U.S., where the population is increasingly becoming racially diverse, simply makes good business sense. Companies that refuse to adapt to the population changes by hiring and promoting persons of color will not be prepared to successfully compete against their competitors in the U.S. or abroad.
- Discrimination will become more increasingly unpopular among whites as the U.S. population becomes more racially diverse and persons of color gain even more economic power. It will not make good business sense for persons of non-color to deny persons of color employment, housing, home mortgage loans, homeowner's insurance, or a membership at the private country club, because the economy will become increasingly more dependent upon their financial investment.

What implications will the U.S. population projections have on the Church as an institution?

- Because of the changes occurring in the U.S. population, churches that primarily consist of persons of non-color will become increasingly elderly and will have to make a greater effort to reach out to persons of color. If these churches decide to reject or ignore the U.S. population projections they could cease to exist or conceivably have a for sale sign outside their doors.

- Since the U.S. is becoming a more racially diverse nation, many more persons of color will be coming through the doors of our nation's churches. The churches that primarily consist of persons of non-color that decide to make a conscious decision to hire and promote persons of color on their staff will be in the best possible position to minister to hurting people and reach their communities.

- Since the U.S. population projections indicate that immigration from Latin America and Asian countries will play a significant role in diversifying the nation, churches will need to consider hiring some staff that are bilingual or that speak a number of languages. Also, language interpreters and the proper translation audio equipment will have to be made available for people who need language interpretation services.

- Since the U.S. population is becoming more racially diverse, it is imperative for churches that primarily consist of persons of non-color to begin examining their church culture and their organizational structures to determine whether or not there are any barriers that would discourage persons of color from visiting or becoming members of their churches.

- Since the racial make up of the U.S. population is going to change substantially in the future, churches that primarily consist of persons from the same racial group will need to consider reaching out and embracing all of God's people.

- Since the U.S. population is aging, there will a greater demand for churches to provide more programming and services for the elderly.

America has refused to come to terms with the issue of race. Our nation's history has been plagued with racial division. The Rodney King beating, Los Angeles riots, O.J. Simpson trial, and the killing of James Byrd, Jr.—an African-American who was dragged by a pick-up truck driven by three white males in Jasper, Texas—has helped to create further racial tensions and polarization in our country.

Former President Bill Clinton recognized that the issue of race in America needed to be addressed at the national level. This is the reason why he attempted to create a national dialogue on the topic of race and created the President's Initiative on Race, which brought together national scholars from across the country to study this issue and make recommendations. The report that the President's Initiative on Race produced, entitled *One America*, noted that while religious leaders have made some efforts to address racial reconciliation, they could do much more if they really wanted to address this issue.[25] The report also states, "Some in the religious community have expressed regret at the clergy's lack of leadership and a desire for them to become more aggressive leaders in this regard."[26]

The secular world has had no choice but to attempt to provide leadership in addressing racial tensions and problems in the United States because the Church as an institution has simply abdicated its responsibility. This is the reason why a good deal of the blame for the current racial climate in this country can be placed at the doorsteps of our nation's churches.

I would have never been able to draft the questions in this book had I never experienced prejudice, bigotry, and racism during my lifetime. Because I have encountered so many persons of non-color that have had a sin problem in this area, it has provided me with a unique opportunity to gain a more profound understanding of the issue. Many persons of color who are believers—and some that are not from the United States—have shared with me their pain and emotional scars that they have suffered as a result of unpleasant experiences in dealing with persons of non-color. A good number of these experiences have occurred from within the four walls of the Church! I have also encountered persons of color who have harbored prejudice and bigotry toward people who come from different races.

I personally have been called a "nigger" on several occasions by persons of non-color. Also, I don't believe that I will ever forget an encounter that I had with a person of non-color who told me that I was on the wrong side of town.

I was bussed to a high school that primarily consisted of persons of non-color after a very successful high school that primarily consisted of persons of color was shut down by the local school board. Several persons of color and persons of non-color were getting ready to riot at my high school until I, along with some other students, walked in the middle of this very explosive situation and stopped it. I still can recall quite vividly that the students at the time were not concerned at all whether or not the dispute was worth coming to blows over; they simply took sides based upon race. Finally, what was so ironic about this potentially explosive situation was that none of the persons of non-color made any effort to assist the persons of color in helping to intervene to break up the dispute among the students.

When I went to attend a Big Ten university in Michigan, it was not long before I discovered that one of my college professors was giving all of the persons of color in his class the same grade (a C) on every paper. The persons of non-color were given A's and B's. It was widely known across campus, while I was attending college, that persons of color were not supposed to be driving around campus late at night or they would be subject to being pulled over by police officers of non-color. I cannot recall how many times my car was pulled over by the campus police for no reason at all.

Police officers on several occasions have also racially profiled me while I have lived in West Michigan. Also, I do not know how many times my wife I have gone out to eat for lunch or dinner and have been seated in the back of the restaurant by a hostess or host of non-color when there was more suitable seating available elsewhere. I have noticed when I go to the shopping mall dressed down and get out of my car, generally if a person of non-color is getting out of their car near me and happens to glance over at me while shutting their door, they will say, "We better lock our doors." However, when I go to the same shopping mall dressed in a suit this never happens.

One incident that I still can recall is when I went out to dinner with a group of persons of color to a restaurant that was quite frequently patronized by persons of non-color. I will never forget how the hostess refused to seat our entire party even though there was seating available. The hostess did eventually provide me with seating after one of the persons in my party offered his seat to me. A waitress did eventually come to take our order after a considerable time had elapsed. Once the waitress did begin to take our order, before she could finish she stormed off. A number of other waitresses working at the restaurant began to walk by our table and glare at the people seated at my table. The waitress did eventually return after a short while, once she regained her composure, to finish taking our order. However, once she glanced over at some persons of non-color that was seated across from my table, she decided to close the divider so they would not have to glance over and look at people who did not look like them. By the way, the food did eventually arrive—forty-five minutes later.

When the waitress closed the divider in the story, it was a good reminder to me how the devil wants to divide people over the issue of race. This is the reason why the Church must not remain silent. God has given each believer of Jesus Christ the ministry of reconciliation. We are supposed to be ambassadors of reconciliation. Pastors must lead the way in mobilizing their churches to address the issues of prejudice, bigotry, and racism. The Church can no longer sit on the sidelines while the devil tries to use the issue of race to drive a wedge between persons of color and persons of non-color.

Why has the church "dropped the ball" when it comes to addressing racism? I have found that it is far worse to deny or ignore a problem than it is to deal with it. Unfortunately, one of the reasons why prejudice, bigotry and racism have persisted for so long in the Church is that pastors of non-color have failed to acknowledge and address this issue from their pulpit. The second reason this problem still continues to persist is that pastors of non-color have allowed pride to fog up their spiritual glasses so that they embrace a "one size fits all" church culture and organizational structure that persons of color do not find to be very appealing.

I am convinced based upon the U.S. becoming a more racially diverse nation that pastors of non-color must begin to make the necessary changes within their churches and be more intentional about reaching out to persons of color. Pastors of non-color must ensure that neither they nor their churches will intentionally or unintentionally perpetuate racism. Beyond making worship services more sensitive to persons of color, I believe that pastors of non-color have to seriously begin to dismantle racism within their churches by hiring and promoting persons of color into significant positions. Pastors of non-color must put to death the practice of simply hiring people on their staff that look and act like them if they desire for their churches to remain culturally relevant in a postmodern world.

I personally have met with and talked to a number of pastors of non-color who told me that they wanted to see their churches have an impact in the urban community. Some of them attempted to establish friendships and partnerships with urban pastors; however, the majority of them simply have found it to be very comforting to simply talk about what they desire to do rather than following their words up with any action.

Unfortunately, so many pastors of color have had to deal with so many empty promises some of them have become very suspicious when they receive a telephone call from a pastor of non-color expressing an interest in developing a friendship and/or a partnership with them.

I always find it to be very interesting when I see pastors of non-color who specifically set aside a good portion of their church budget to support missionary projects overseas but don't make the same effort when it comes to the urban community. Unfortunately, the majority of pastors of non-color have never spent enough time in the urban community to really understand what the needs are so they could effectively minister to all of God's people. Also, these pastors of non-color and their churches have missed out on some wonderful opportunities to partner with pastors of color because they have set up too many conditions that must be met before they will consider doing anything.

When Jesus walked upon the earth, He took care of the physical needs of the people as well as their spiritual needs. Perhaps some of us have simply forgotten how Jesus ministered to hurting people. I do not recall Jesus telling people that He encountered in the Scriptures that they would first have to jump through at least twenty to thirty hoops before He would show any compassion and minister to them.

Pastors of color should not allow the prejudice, bigotry, and racism that they have experienced in the past to cause them to make the assumption that no pastors of non-color can be trusted. Because they may have had some unpleasant experiences in establishing friendships with pastors of non-color in the past, a number of pastors of color have no desire—or simply gave up on—trying to develop friendships with them along time ago. As a result, some pastors of color have simply decided to establish close friendships with fellow pastors from the same race. Pastors of color that make the decision to isolate themselves and their congregations from pastors of non-color and their congregations do nothing to foster unity within the body.

Pastors of color are tired of simply talking about the issues of race and inequality they want to see some substantial progress being made in addressing prejudice, bigotry, and racism. For far too long, pastors of color have had to take on these very tough issues without very little help from pastors of non-color and their churches. Unfortunately, the vast majority of these pastors of non-color and their churches have either chosen to deny that there was a problem, ignore the problem, or have refused to do anything about the problem.

America needs to repent of the sins of prejudice, bigotry, and racism. I am convinced that the answer to our nation's racial problems and tensions can only be found through confession, repentance, and forgiveness. We need to confess our sins, repent, and ask God to forgive us and heal our land. Otherwise, America could experience racial conflict as it never has before—given the projected changes in the U.S. population.

ABC News released the findings of a poll they conducted on Monday, October 5, 1999, that revealed what Americans believed would be the greatest challenges in the new millennium. The findings of the poll revealed that fourteen percent of those surveyed felt that prejudice and racism would be the major challenges, and nine percent of those polled felt that people needed to learn how to get along with one another.[27] The poll also noted that prejudice and racism were selected with the same frequency among whites as well as blacks. The issues of the prejudice and racism were ranked by those being surveyed ahead of other concerns such as pollution, violence, overpopulation, war, immorality, and food shortages.

Jesus Christ will soon return for a bride without spot or wrinkle on her garment. Unfortunately, the terrible stains of prejudice, bigotry, and racism have not yet been removed from the bride's garment. I know that in my own life it has not always been easy to bring people together from diverse racial and cultural backgrounds. In my efforts to bring healing to broken and fractured relationships, I have suffered great joy and a lot of pain. Oftentimes, my enthusiasm and compassion for seeing people from diverse racial and cultural backgrounds come together for God's glory has turned some people off, made others very uncomfortable, caused me to often be misunderstood, provided some with the opportunity to question my motives, given others a reason to distance themselves from me and caused others to criticize me or even attempt to humiliate me. However, I have refused to run away from or to completely abandon the very thing that God has commissioned me to do!

I remember being taunted when I was growing up as a child in a predominantly African-American neighborhood and made fun by other children in my neighborhood because I decided to invite one of my friends over to my house to play—who happened to be a person of non-color. Also, I remember an experience that I had at one of the largest malls in the United States. After selecting a restaurant to eat at, I asked the waiter if my wife and I could be seated in the non-smoking section. The waiter, after parading us by the persons of non-color and plenty of empty seats in the restaurant, took us to a separate room that was completely empty to be seated. Of course, we chose to leave the restaurant and as good stewards invest our money elsewhere.

Once, I worked on a major evangelistic outreach event. I was invited to attend a meeting where the committee was going to have to decide whether or not a person of color should be allowed to continue to work on the event. I was waiting for credible information to be provided as to why this person should not be allowed to continue to serve. One of the committee members commented that the person of color was "different, slick," and even suggested that perhaps the person's cultural background would not make the person a "good team player." These were only a few of the racially insensitive reasons that were given for preventing the person of color from serving on a committee.

I remember attending a church that primarily consisted of persons of color that came from the same racial background where the some of the people would laugh whenever a person of non-color came forward to receive salvation or become a member of the church. This always bothered me, because these individuals should have been rejoicing rather than laughing! They chose to behave this way because the person that came forward was from a different racial or cultural background.

I still recall walking into a gas station in Georgia and hearing the persons of non-color who worked there begin to tell racial jokes and laugh out loud. Why did I have to endure such harassment? I simply wanted to pay for my gas.

Also, I once had an encounter with an elderly gentleman that was quite memorable and comical. The man who happened to be a person of non-color approached me and apparently wanted to say hello. I immediately noticed that he seemed nervous and very uncomfortable. The man kept nodding his head at me as he attempted to give me a handshake in the same manner that persons of color will on occasion greet one another. To give you a better visual: Do you remember the Flip Wilson's comedy show that use to air on television during the 70's? Flip used to playfully joke by slapping hands, elbows and doing the bump with some of his guests? Beyond the handshake, I was more concerned about whether the gentleman would actually try and pull the old Flip Wilson routine on me! Apparently, the man believed based upon a racial stereotype that this was how he was supposed to shake hands with a person of color.

God not only gives every believer the ministry of reconciliation, but His Word declares that believers have supernaturally been given the message of reconciliation (2 Corinthians 5:19). In other words, believers have not only been given a ministry, but they have been given a message that can repair broken and fractured relationships. It would have been terrible if God would have given us a ministry without a message! This powerful life-changing message can be found in the Gospel of Jesus Christ. This message surpasses racial or cultural barriers and leads to genuine reconciliation.

God has given each believer 1) the ministry of reconciliation, 2) the message of reconciliation, and 3) and the appointed office of ambassador (2 Corinthians 5:20). Random House Dictionary defines an ambassador as being a diplomatic official of the highest rank. God has appointed every believer to serve as an ambassador on behalf of His Son, Jesus Christ! God has given each believer a ministry, a message, and a diplomatic assignment as ambassador. Believers (ambassadors) should always seek to repair broken and fractured relationships by reaching out to those who have been hurt, wounded, or even discarded by society.

I have seen how God can take persons of color that have experienced bigotry, prejudice, and racism and use them as ambassadors to bring healing to the Body of Christ. Also, I have seen God use these ambassadors to speak out against racial injustices and as powerful instruments of reconciliation.

Bob Woodrick, the Chairman of D & W Food Centers based in Grand Rapids, Michigan, has used his power, wealth, and influence to speak out against racism. He also has created the Woodrick Institute for the Study of Racism and has encouraged others to speak out against and take action to address racism.

Dr. Ed Dobson, the senior pastor of Calvary Church—also based in Grand Rapids, Michigan—taught a four-week series on the topic of racism at his church that was televised throughout the West Michigan area. He has played a very instrumental role in having his church establish partnerships with urban churches.

For several years, more than seven hundred people have come together to attend a Summit on Racism in Grand Rapids, Michigan to discuss the issue of racism and formulate action plans to address the problem. These meetings have been convened by Grand Rapids Area Center for Ecumenism's Racial Justice Institute (RJI). Reverend David May, the executive director of RJI, should be commended for conceptualizing and implementing such a worthwhile event, which has had a very positive impact on West Michigan.

Dr. Fred Price the senior pastor of Crenshaw Christian Center, based in Los Angeles, California, chose not to remain silent on this issue by using his nationally-televised program to address the issue of racism in the Church. Dr. Price should also be commended for taking the national platform that God has given him to definitively address this topic.

It has been wonderful to see the Promise Keepers Ministry making the issue of racial reconciliation a major priority at their meetings, which have been held across United States and around the globe. Coach Bill McCartney the Chairman of Promise Keepers has spent a great deal of his time speaking out against racism and challenging men to address racism and become ambassadors of racial healing within their churches and communities.

Scott Hagan, the senior pastor of Grand Rapids First Assembly, has made a very serious effort to make the diversity that is found in the cross of Jesus Christ a reality at his church. I believe that Grand Rapids First Assembly of God Church will become a national model for the world to see how how a church that primarily consisted of persons of non-color can successfully transition into becoming a multi-ethnic church that looks like heaven.

God can use anyone who is willing to be used as an ambassador to help bring racial healing to broken and fractured relationships. Genuine peace and unity can only be found in Jesus Christ, the common thread that holds the beautiful colorful fabric that represents the racial and ethnic diversity of our nation together.

══════APPENDIXES══════

APPENDIX A

Consultants and Referral Sources

Diversity and Racism-Related Issues for Businesses:

Advanced Research Management Consultants (ARMC)
Address: 1014 South Second St.
                  Philadelphia, PA 19147
Contact Person: John P. Fernandez, Ph.D.
Phone: (800) 237-9856
Fax: (215) 551-3710
Web site: www.armc-hr.com
E-mail: j.fernandez@att.net

Diversity Management Strategists
Address: 751 Kenmoor Ave. SE, Suite F
                  Grand Rapids, MI 49546
Contact Person: Tom Mecher, Partner and Skot Welch, Senior Advisor
Phone: (616) 575-8122
Fax: (616) 575-7775
Web site: www.dmstrategists.com
E-mail: swelch@dmstrategists.com or tmecher@dmstrategists.com

Gaines & Associates, Inc.
Address: 2658 Carlton NE
                  Grand Rapids, MI 49505
Contact Person: Gwen Gaines-Mofitt
Phone: (616) 363-3113
Fax: (616) 363-3272
Web site: Not Available
E-mail: diverseg@iserv.net

Grand Rapids Area Chamber of Commerce

Address: 111 Pearl St. NW
                 Grand Rapids, MI 49503-2831
Contact Person: Sonya Hughes, Diversity Programs Director
Phone: (616) 771-0300
Fax: (616) 771-0318
Web site: www.grandrapids.org
E-mail: hughess@grandrapids.org

Inclusive Business Strategies, Inc.

Address: 819 Harbor Bend Rd.
                 Memphis, TN 38103
Contact Person: Rachelle Hood-Phillips
Phone: (901) 529-8728
Fax: (901) 529-8727
Web site: Not Available
E-mail: r-hoodthi@midsouth.rr.com

Santiago Solutions Group

Address: 1487 Noe Street
                 San Francisco, CA 94131
Contact Persons: Carlos Santiago, President & C.E.O. and Isabel Valdes,
                 Senior Advisor
Phone: (415) 206-9318
Fax: (415) 206-9320
Web site: www.santiagovaldessolutions.com
E-mail: info@santiagovaldessolutions.com

The American Institute for Managing Diversity

Address: 50 Hurt Plaza, Suite 1150
                 Atlanta, GA 30303
Contact Person: Dr. R. Roosevelt Thomas, Jr., D.B.A., Senior Research
                 Fellow & Founder
Phone: (404) 302-9226
Fax: (404) 302-9252
Web site: www.aimd.org
E-mail: RRThomasJr@aol.com

Upton Consulting
Address: P.O. Box 1351
                   Grand Rapids, MI 49501-1351
Contact Persons: Robert or Sandra Upton, Senior Consultants
Phone: (616) 243-5129
Web site: Not Available
E-mail: rsuptongr@aol.com

SuccessSource
Address: 2940 Noble Road, Suite 103
                   Cleveland Heights, Ohio 44121
Contact Person: George C. Fraser, President
Phone: (216) 691-6686
Fax: (216) 691-6685
Web site: www.frasernet.com
E-mail: gfraser@frasernet.com

Woodrick Institute for the Study of Racism and Diversity
Address: 1607 Robinson Rd. SE
                   Grand Rapids, MI 49506
Contact Person: Steve L. Robbins, Ph.D., Director
Phone: (616) 459-8281 ext. 4464
Fax: (616) 459-2653
Web site: www.woodrickinstitute.org
E-mail: robbiste@aquinas.edu

Diversity and Racism-Related Issues for Churches & Parachurch Ministries:

Crossroads Ministry—National Office
Address: 425 S. Central Park Ave.
                   Chicago, IL 60624
Contact Person: Reverend Joseph Barndt, Director
Phone: (773) 638-0166
Fax: (773) 638-0167
Web site: www.crossroadsigc.org
E-mail: crossroads@igc.org

Grand Rapids Area Center for Ecumenism

Address: Racial Justice Institute
                    207 E. Fulton, 4th floor
                    Grand Rapids, MI 49503
Contact Person: Reverend David May, Director
Phone: (616) 774-2042
Fax: (616) 774-2883
Web site: www.grmc.org/grace/
E-mail: dmay@graceoffice.org

John M. Perkins Foundation for Reconciliation & Development

Address: 1831 Robinson St.
                    Jackson, Mississippi 39209
Contact Person: Dr. John Perkins, President
Phone: (601) 354-1563
Fax: (601) 352-6882
Web site: www.jmpf.org
E-mail: jmpfoffice@aol.com

National Council of Churches

Address: 475 Riverside Dr., Rm. 880
                    New York, NY 10115
Phone: (212) 870-2511
Fax: (212) 870-2030
Web site: www.nccusa.org
E-mail: news@nccusa.org

Reconciliation Ministries International

Address: 1111 Wood St.
                    Pittsburgh, PA 15221
Contact Person: Pastor Sanford Cooper, Pastoral Executive Director
Phone: (412) 244-9494
Fax: (412) 244-9655
Web site: www.reconciliationintl.com
E-mail: Sanfordcooper@Charter.Net

Upton Consulting

Address:	P.O. Box 1351
	Grand Rapids, MI 49501-1351
Contact Persons:	Robert and Sandra Upton, Senior Consultants
Phone:	(616) 243-5129
Web site:	Not Available
E-mail:	rsuptongr@aol.com

Special Focus on Native Americans:

Eagles Wings Ministry

Address	1580 Marvin Adcock Rd.
	Hayden, AL 35079
Contact Person:	Randy Woodley, President
Phone:	(205) 559-8100
Fax:	(205) 559-8009
Web site:	www.eagles-wingsmin.com
E-mail:	rw@eagles-wingsmin.com

Wiconi International

Address	P.O. Box 5246
	Vancouver, WA 98668
Contact Person:	Richard Twiss
Phone:	(360) 546-1867
Fax:	(360) 546-3801
Web site:	www.wiconi.com
E-mail:	wanbli@aol.com

National League of Cities
Address: 1301 Pennsylvania Ave. NW, Suite 550
                  Washington, D.C. 20004-1763
Contact Person: Don Borut, Executive Director
Phone: (202) 626-3000
Fax: (202) 626-3043
Web site: www.nlc.org
E-mail: borut@nlc.org or vanetten@nlc.org

General Population and Other Statistical Data Regarding Race and Ethnicity:

U.S. Census Bureau
Address: Washington, D.C. 20233
Phone: (301) 457-4698
Web site: www.census.gov
E-mail: Population statistics - pop@census.gov Income, poverty,
                  housing, labor force, occupations statistics - hhes-info@cen-
                  sus.gov International statistics - ipc@census.gov

APPENDIX B

*Ten Best Practices for Establishing
Cross-Cultural Friendships/Relationships*

1. Be willing to be intentional about establishing a strong friendship/relationship.
2. Be willing to invest the necessary time in developing a strong friendship/relationship.
3. Be willing to become vulnerable with one another.
4. Be willing to value what you have in common with one another.
5. Be willing to value what you do not have in common with one another.
6. Be willing to forgive one another.
7. Be willing to pray and intercede for one another.
8. Be willing to learn from one another.
9. Be willing to sharpen one another as friends.
10. Be willing to appreciate the other person's life journey and testimony.

APPENDIX C

Ten Best Practices for Developing Racially Diverse
Organizations that Are Representative of God's Kingdom

1. Require the leader of the organization and appropriate staff persons as part of their job responsibilities to make significant progress in hiring, promoting and creating business opportunities for persons of color.
2. Recruit persons of color for the policy-making board and various advisory teams of the organization.
3. Examine the organizational culture (values, belief system) to determine whether or not any barriers exist that may impede efforts to recruit, hire and promote persons of color.
4. Develop a strategic plan to ensure that persons of color are valued and encouraged to contribute their gifts and talents to the success of the organization. This plan should be reviewed and updated on a regular basis.
5. Recruit, hire, and promote persons of color to work at all levels of the organization.
6. Make the necessary adjustments within the organization to obtain racial diversity. Also, develop strategic alliances with other organizations that promote racial unity and address racism.
7. Remove any barriers—written or unwritten policies, procedures, practices, organizational structure or the corporate culture impediments— that inhibit persons of color from being recruited, hired, promoted, and valued.
8. Provide businesses owned by persons of color with vendor service opportunities, contracting opportunities, and professional service consulting opportunities.
9. Reward employees that make significant progress in recruiting, hiring and promoting persons of color within the organization. Also, employees should be rewarded for demonstrating success in creating business opportunities for persons of color.
10. Develop a zero tolerance for racial prejudice, bigotry and racism within the organization. Also, facilitate employee small group discussions that examine racial diversity-related issues on a regular basis.

APPENDIX D

Self-Assessment Tool

■ What goal(s) will you set to foster greater racial unity among believers?

_____

_____

_____

_____

_____

■ What action steps will you take to reach your goal(s)? _____

_____

_____

_____

_____

_____

■ What are the anticipated completion date(s)? _____

_____

_____

_____

_____

_____

■ How will you measure progress made? _____

_____

_____

_____

_____

_____

■ What person(s) will hold you accountable?_____

_____

_____

_____

_____

■ How have your experiences helped you to grow spiritually? _____

_____

_____

_____

_____

_____

*   Taken from *Racism@Work Among the LORD's People* 2003 Robert Upton. Permission granted to photocopy for personal or group use.

APPENDIX E

Definition of Terms

Persons of Color: refers to persons that come from any of the following racial/ethnic groups: American Indian or Alaska Native; Asian; Black or African American; Native Hawaiian and Pacific Islander. The term persons of color is used throughout the book rather than racial minorities.

Persons of Non-Color: refers to persons from the White population.

Prejudice: to have opinions without knowing the facts and to hold onto the opinions, even after contrary facts are known.

Bigotry: to vigorously resist an alternate point of view based upon distorted racial biases.

Racism: goes beyond prejudice. It is backed up by power. Racism is the power to enforce one's prejudices. This can be practiced by individuals or institutions. Institutions that possess power can perpetuate racism (intentional or unintentional) through their personnel, policies, practices, structures and foundations that subordinate or exploit people of color

<u>**Special Note:**</u> The population projections for the United States that have been included in the book are based upon U.S. Census Bureau middle-series projections rather than lower or higher-series projections. Population projections for the United States are always subject to change based upon any

unforeseen events or variations in fertility, life expectancy or net immigration.

Special permission has been granted by Augsburg Fortress to include the above definitions for the terms prejudice, bigotry and racism that were excerpted from Dismantling Racism by Joseph Barndt.

APPENDIX F

Prejudiced, Bigoted, and Racist Thoughts / Statements

The following thoughts being acted upon or verbal comments made by pastors, church leaders, church staff, lay members, denominational leaders, or staff may be a good indicator of whether or not their hearts have been infected by prejudice, bigotry, or racism:

Prejudice

- I am afraid of you.
- I am superior to you.
- I cannot trust you.
- I do not feel that comfortable around you.
- You will need my help.
- You must need something from me.
- I don't need you.
- You must have an agenda.
- You are not welcome here.
- It would probably be better if you find another church to attend.
- I really do not want to get to know you.
- I do not want my church or denomination to have to change the way that it does ministry in order to accommodate you.
- I will only tolerate you.
- I will not celebrate you.
- I don't want to change in order for you to be here.
- I don't want to have to learn the lyrics of new songs and get used to new music in order to have you here.
- If my church or denomination changes too much in an effort to reach out to persons of color, then I am going to leave.
- I will leave if too many persons of color start attending my church.
- I do not like their kind of music.
- The music that they like to listen to is too loud.

Bigotry

- If too many persons of color attend my church then we will have to spend more money trying to address their financial needs.
- Most persons of color are very emotional.
- Most persons of color are very liberal when it comes to moral issues.
- The persons of color will not contribute much financially to the church.
- The majority of persons of color are on welfare or some form of public assistance.
- All persons of color can sing and dance.

Racism

- I am not going to hire any persons of color to be on my church or denominational staff.
- If I have to hire a person of color, then I am going to hire a person that will think and act like me.
- I do not want any persons of color on the policy-making board.
- I will make sure if any persons of color do become part of the policy-making board that they will not outnumber the persons of non-color.
- I will make sure that if any new policy changes are made that they will primarily benefit the persons of non-color.
- I will make sure that the corporate culture of my church does not change.
- I will make sure that my church only hires companies that are owned by persons of non-color as vendors, suppliers, professional service consultants, and construction contractors.
- I do not want the persons of color to eventually outnumber the persons of non-color at my church.
- I do not want to make any changes or too many changes at my church or denomination because the persons of non-color may leave.
- I will maintain control over how much persons of color are able to use their gifts and talents at my church.

- I will make sure the financial resources designated for church mission efforts are targeted toward overseas mission efforts rather than urban ministry initiatives.
- I will make sure that all or a majority of guest ministers or special guests that come to my church will be persons of non-color.
- I will refuse to make any changes in the worship songs and music at my church in order to more effectively reach out to persons of color.
- I will plant churches in suburban communities or overseas rather than in the urban community.

SUGGESTED READING

America Becoming: Racial Trends and Their Consequences, Volume 1. National Research Council Washington, D.C.: National Academy Press, 2001.

America Becoming: Racial Trends and Their Consequences, Volume 2. National Research Council Washington, D.C.: National Academy Press. 2001.

America's Original Sin: A Study on White Racism. Washington, D.C.: Sojourners, 1992.

Evangelism That Works. Barna, George. Ventura, California: Regal Books, 1995.

The Frog in the Kettle. Barna, George. Ventura, California: Regal Books, 1990.

The Leading Index of Leading Spiritual Indicators. Barna, George. Dallas, Texas: Word Publishing, 1996.

What Americans Believe. Barna, George. Ventura, California: Regal Books, 1991.

The Second Coming of the Church. Barna, George. Nashville, Tennessee: Word Publishing, 1998.

Dismantling Racism. Barndt, Joseph. Minneapolis, Minnesota: Augsburg Fortress, 1991.

Fulfilling the Dream. Branding, Ronice. St. Louis, Missouri: Chalice Press, 1998.

Building Unity in the Church of the New Millennium. Chicago, Illinois: Moody Press, 2002.

Futuring. Chand, Samuel R. and Cecil Murphey. Grand Rapids, Michigan: Baker Books, 2002.

Council of Economic Advisers for the President's Initiative on Race. Washington, D.C.: 1998.

Color Blind. Cose, Ellis. New York, New York: HarperCollins Publishers, 1997.

Ending Racism in the Church. Davies, Susan E. and Sister Paul Teresa Hennessee, S.A. Cleveland, OH: United Church Press, 1998.

Reconciliation. DeYoung, Curtiss Paul. Valley Forge, Pennsylvania: Judson Press, 1997.

The Leader of the Future. Drucker Foundation. San Francisco, California: Jossey-Bass Publishers, 1996.

The Organization of the Future. Drucker Foundation. San Francisco, California: Jossey-Bass Publishers, 1997.

The Community of the Future. Drucker Foundation. San Francisco, California: Jossey-Bass Publishers, 1998.

Leader to Leader. Drucker Foundation. San Francisco, California: Jossey-Bass Publishers, 1999.

The Routledge Atlas of African American History. Earle, Jonathan. New York, New York: Routledge, 2000.

Growing Spiritual Redwoods. Easum, William M. and Thomas G. Bandy. Nashville, Tennessee: Abingdon Press, 1997.

Leadership on the Other Side. Easum, William M. Nashville, Tennessee: Abingdon Press, 2000.

Purging Racism from Christianity. Edwards, Jr., Jefferson D. Grand Rapids, Michigan: Zondervan Publishing House, 1996.

Let's Get to Know Each Other. Evans, Dr. Tony. Nashville, Tennessee: Thomas Nelson, Inc., 1995.

Racist America. Feagin, Joe R. New York, New York: Routledge, 2000.

The First R. Feagin, Joe R. and Debra Van Ausdale. Lanham, Maryland: Rowman & Littlefield Publishers, Inc., 2001.

White Racism. Feagin, Joe R. and Hernan Vera. New York, New York: Routledge, 1995.

Race, Racism and the Biblical Narratives. Felder, Cain Hope. Minneapolis, Minnesota: Augsburg Fortress, 2002.

Race, Gender & Rhetoric. Fernandez, John P. New York, New York: McGraw-Hill, 1998.

Managing a Diverse Work Force. Fernandez, John P. Lexington, Massachusetts: Lexington Books, 1991.

Right or Reconciled? Garlington, Joseph L. Shippensburg, Pennsylvania: Destiny Image, 1998.

They Walked with the Savior. Hagan, Scott. Lake Mary, Florida: Charisma House, 2002.

One Blood. Ham, Ken, Carl Wieland and Don Batten. Green Forest, Arizona: 1999.

The Racial Problem in Christian Perspective. Haselden, Kyle. New York, New York: Harper & Brothers Publishers, 1959.

Hesselbein on Leadership. Hesselbein, Frances. San Francisco, California: Jossey-Bass Publishers, 2002.

Becoming a Contagious Christian. Hybels, Bill and Mark Mittelberg. Grand Rapids, Michigan: Zondervan Publishing House, 1994.

Here Comes the Bride. Hutcherson, Ken. Sisters, Oregon: Multnomah Publishers, 2000.

What Color Is Your God? Ireland, David. Verona, New Jersey: Impact Publishing House, 2000.

Overcoming Racism. Joyner, Rick. Charlotte, North Carolina: Morningstar Publications, 1996.

Uprooting Racism. Kivel, Paul. Philadelphia, Pennsylvania: New Society Publishers, 1996.

The Upside Down Church. Laurie, Greg. Wheaton, Illinois: Tyndale House Publishers, Inc., 1999.

American Apartheid. Massey, Douglas S., and Nancy A. Denton. London, England: Harvard University Press, 1993.

Developing the Leaders Around You. Maxwell, John. Nashville, Tennessee: Thomas Nelson Publishers, 1995.

Developing the Leader Within You. Maxwell, John. Nashville, Tennessee: Thomas Nelson, 1993.

A New Kind of Christian. McLaren, Brian D. San Francisco, California: Jossey-Bass Publishers, 2001.

The Church on the Other Side. McLaren, Brian D. Grand Rapids, Michigan: Zondervan Publishing House, 2000.

Minorities. San Diego, California: Greenhaven Press, 1998.

Showing My Color. Page, Clarence. New York, New York: HarperCollins Publishers, 1996.

One Blood. Paulk, Earl. Shippensburg, Pennsylvania: Destiny Image, 1996.

Restoring At-Risk Communities. Perkins, John. Grand Rapids, Michigan: Baker Books, 1995.

He's My Brother. Perkins, John, Thomas A. Tarrants, and David Winbush. Grand Rapids, Michigan: Chosen Books, 1994.

More than Equals. Perkins, Spencer and Chris Rice. Downers Grove, Illinois: InterVarsity Press, 1993.

Building Unity in the Church. Perry, Dwight. Chicago, Illinois: Moody Press, 2002.

Separate No More. Pert, Norman Anthony. Grand Rapids, Michigan: Baker Books, 2000.

Cultural Change & Your Church. Pocock, Michael and Joseph Henriques. Grand Rapids, Michigan: Baker Books, 2002.

Let the Walls Fall Down. Porter, Phillip. Lake Mary, Florida: Creation House, 1996.

President's Initiative on Race. One America in the 21st Century. Washington, D.C.: The White House, 1998.

Racism. San Diego, California: Greenhaven, 1998.

Healing Racism in America. Rutstein, Nathan. Springfield, Massachusetts: Whitcomb Publishers, 1993.

Racism: Unraveling the Fear. Rutstein, Nathan. Washington, D.C.: The Global Classroom, 1997.

Racial and Ethnic Groups. Schaefer, Richardson T. New York, New York: Addison-Wesley Educational Publishers, Inc., 1998.

Discontinuity and Hope. Schaller, Lyle E. Nashville, Tennessee: Abingdon Press, 1999.

What Have We Learned? Schaller, Lyle E. Nashville, Tennessee: Abingdon Press, 2001.

Winning The Race. Schuler, Clarence F. Chicago, Illinois: Moody Press, 1998.

Beyond Race and Gender. Thomas, Jr., R. Roosevelt. New York, New York: American Management Association, 1991.

Theological Resources for Racial Reconciliation. Westmont, Illinois: InterVarsity Press, 1997.

One Church Many Tribes. Twiss, Richard. Ventura, California: Regal Books, 2000.

Population Projections of the United States by Age, Race, and Hispanic Origin: 1995 to 2050. U.S. Department of Commerce's Bureau of the Census. Report No. P25-1130. Washington, D.C.: 1996.

We the American Asians. U.S. Department of Commerce's Bureau of the Census. Washington, D.C.: 1993.

We the American Blacks U.S. Department of Commerce's Bureau of the Census. Washington, D.C.: 1993.

We the American Hispanics. U.S. Department of Commerce's Bureau of the Census. Washington, D.C.: 1993.

We the American Pacific Islanders. U.S. Department of Commerce's Bureau of the Census. Washington, D.C.: 1993.

We the First Americans. U.S. Department of Commerce's Bureau of the Census. Washington, DC.: 1993.

Face to Face. Waller, James. New York, New York: Plenum Press, 1998.

Faith Works. Wallis, Jim. New York, New York: Random House, 2000.

Prejudice and the People of God. Ware, A. Charles. Grand Rapids, Michigan: Kregel Publications, 2001.

Breaking Down Walls. Washington, Raleigh and Glen Kehrem. Chicago, Illinois: Moody Press, 1993.

The Purpose Driven Church. Warren, Rick. Grand Rapids, Michigan: Zondervan Publishing House, 1995.

The Bridge Over the Racial Divide. Wilson, William Julius. Berkley, California: University of California Press: 1999.

Living in Color. Woodley, Randy. Grand Rapids, Michigan: Chosen Books, 2001.

Beyond Black and White. Yancey, George A., Grand Rapids, Michigan: Baker Books, 1996.

Scriptures for Your Heart

Did you know that the word heart is referenced 545 times in the Bible? Please allow the following Bible Scripture verses to penetrate your heart:

Genesis 6:5	Exodus 28:29	Deuteronomy 15:10
Genesis 6:6	Exodus 28:30	Deuteronomy 17:17
Genesis 8:21	Exodus 35:21	Deuteronomy 20:3
Genesis 24:45	Leviticus 6:9	Deuteronomy 20:8
Genesis 34:3	Leviticus 19:17	Deuteronomy 26:16
Genesis 34:8	Leviticus 26:36	Deuteronomy 28:65
Genesis 42:28	Leviticus 26:41	Deuteronomy 28:67
Exodus 4:14	Numbers 14:24	Deuteronomy 29:18
Exodus 4:21	Numbers 15:39	Deuteronomy 30:1
Exodus 7:3	Numbers 32:11	Deuteronomy 30:2
Exodus 7:13	Numbers 32:12	Deuteronomy 30:6
Exodus 7:14	Deuteronomy 1:28	Deuteronomy 30:10
Exodus 7:22	Deuteronomy 1:36	Deuteronomy 30:14
Exodus 7:23	Deuteronomy 2:30	Deuteronomy 30:17
Exodus 8:15	Deuteronomy 4:9	Deuteronomy 32:46
Exodus 8:19	Deuteronomy 4:29	Joshua 2:11
Exodus 8:32	Deuteronomy 4:39	Joshua 5:1
Exodus 9:7	Deuteronomy 5:29	Joshua 7:5
Exodus 9:12	Deuteronomy 6:5	Joshua 11:20
Exodus 9:34	Deuteronomy 6:6	Joshua 14:8
Exodus 9:35	Deuteronomy 8:2	Joshua 14:9
Exodus 10:1	Deuteronomy 8:5	Joshua 14:14
Exodus 10:20	Deuteronomy 8:14	Joshua 22:5
Exodus 10:27	Deuteronomy 10:12	Joshua 23:14
Exodus 11:10	Deuteronomy 10:16	Joshua 24:23
Exodus 14:4	Deuteronomy 11:3	Judges 5:9
Exodus 14:8	Deuteronomy 11:13	Judges 5:15
Exodus 14:17	Deuteronomy 11:18	Judges 5:16
Exodus 15:8	Deuteronomy 13:3	1 Samuel 1:8
Exodus 25:2	Deuteronomy 15:7	1 Samuel 1:13

1 Samuel 2:1	1 Kings 8:38	2 Chronicles 6:14
1 Samuel 2:33	1 Kings 8:39	2 Chronicles 6:30
1 Samuel 2:35	1 Kings 8:47	2 Chronicles 6:37
1 Samuel 4:13	1 Kings 8:48	2 Chronicles 6:38
1 Samuel 6:6	1 Kings 8:58	2 Chronicles 7:10
1 Samuel 7:3	1 Kings 8:61	2 Chronicles 7:16
1 Samuel 9:19	1 Kings 8:66	2 Chronicles 9:23
1 Samuel 10:9	1 Kings 9:3	2 Chronicles 11:16
1 Samuel 10:26	1 Kings 9:4	2 Chronicles 12:14
1 Samuel 12:20	1 Kings 10:24	2 Chronicles 15:12
1 Samuel 12:24	1 Kings 11:2	2 Chronicles 15:15
1 Samuel 13:14	1 Kings 11:4	2 Chronicles 15:17
1 Samuel 14:7	1 Kings 11:9	2 Chronicles 16:9
1 Samuel 16:7	1 Kings 11:37	2 Chronicles 17:6
1 Samuel 17:28	1 Kings 14:8	2 Chronicles 19:3
1 Samuel 17:32	1 Kings 15:3	2 Chronicles 19:9
1 Samuel 21:12	1 Kings 15:14	2 Chronicles 20:33
1 Samuel 25:37	1 Kings 18:37	2 Chronicles 22:9
1 Samuel 28:5	2 Kings 9:24	2 Chronicles 25:2
2 Samuel 3:21	2 Kings 10:31	2 Chronicles 29:31
2 Samuel 6:16	2 Kings 20:3	2 Chronicles 30:19
2 Samuel 13:20	2 Kings 22:19	2 Chronicles 31:21
2 Samuel 14:1	2 Kings 23:3	2 Chronicles 32:25
2 Samuel 15:6	2 Kings 23:25	2 Chronicles 32:26
2 Samuel 15:13	1 Chronicles 15:29	2 Chronicles 32:31
2 Samuel 17:10	1 Chronicles 16:10	2 Chronicles 34:27
2 Samuel 18:14	1 Chronicles 22:7	2 Chronicles 34:31
2 Samuel 19:14	1 Chronicles 22:19	2 Chronicles 36:13
2 Samuel 22:46	1 Chronicles 28:2	2 Chronicles 36:22
1 Kings 2:4	1 Chronicles 28:9	Ezra 1:1
1 Kings 2:44	1 Chronicles 29:9	Ezra 1:5
1 Kings 3:6	1 Chronicles 29:17	Ezra 7:27
1 Kings 3:9	1 Chronicles 29:18	Nehemiah 2:2
1 Kings 3:12	1 Chronicles 29:19	Nehemiah 2:12
1 Kings 8:17	2 Chronicles 1:11	Nehemiah 4:6
1 Kings 8:18	2 Chronicles 6:7	Nehemiah 7:5
1 Kings 8:23	2 Chronicles 6:8	Nehemiah 9:8

Job 1:5	Psalm 19:14	Psalm 49:3
Job 10:13	Psalm 20:4	Psalm 51:10
Job 11:13	Psalm 21:2	Psalm 51:17
Job 15:12	Psalm 22:14	Psalm 53:1
Job 17:11	Psalm 22:26	Psalm 55:4
Job 19:27	Psalm 24:4	Psalm 55:21
Job 22:22	Psalm 25:17	Psalm 57:7
Job 23:16	Psalm 26:2	Psalm 58:2
Job 29:13	Psalm 27:3	Psalm 61:2
Job 31:7	Psalm 27:8	Psalm 62:4
Job 31:9	Psalm 27:14	Psalm 62:8
Job 31:20	Psalm 28:3	Psalm 62:10
Job 31:27	Psalm 28:7	Psalm 64:6
Job 31:33	Psalm 30:12	Psalm 64:10
Job 33:3	Psalm 31:24	Psalm 66:18
Job 36:13	Psalm 32:11	Psalm 69:20
Job 37:1	Psalm 33:11	Psalm 69:32
Job 37:24	Psalm 33:15	Psalm 73:1
Job 38:36	Psalm 33:21	Psalm 73:7
Psalm 4:4	Psalm 34:18	Psalm 73:13
Psalm 4:7	Psalm 36:1	Psalm 73:21
Psalm 5:9	Psalm 36:10	Psalm 73:26
Psalm 7:9	Psalm 37:4	Psalm 74:8
Psalm 7:10	Psalm 37:15	Psalm 77:6
Psalm 9:1	Psalm 37:31	Psalm 78:8
Psalm 10:3	Psalm 38:8	Psalm 78:37
Psalm 11:2	Psalm 38:10	Psalm 78:72
Psalm 13:2	Psalm 39:3	Psalm 81:12
Psalm 13:5	Psalm 40:8	Psalm 84:2
Psalm 14:1	Psalm 40:10	Psalm 84:5
Psalm 15:2	Psalm 40:12	Psalm 86:11
Psalm 16:7	Psalm 41:6	Psalm 86:12
Psalm 16:9	Psalm 44:18	Psalm 89:50
Psalm 17:3	Psalm 44:21	Psalm 90:12
Psalm 17:10	Psalm 45:1	Psalm 94:15
Psalm 18:45	Psalm 45:5	Psalm 95:8
Psalm 19:8	Psalm 46:2	Psalm 95:10

Psalm 97:11

Psalm 101:2

Psalm 101:4

Psalm 101:5

Psalm 102:4

Psalm 104:15

Psalm 105:3

Psalm 105:25

Psalm 108:1

Psalm 109:16

Psalm 109:22

Psalm 111:1

Psalm 112:7

Psalm 112:8

Psalm 116:6

Psalm 119:2

Psalm 119:7

Psalm 119:10

Psalm 119:11

Psalm 119:30

Psalm 119:32

Psalm 119:34

Psalm 119:36

Psalm 119:58

Psalm 119:69

Psalm 119:70

Psalm 119:80

Psalm 119:111

Psalm 119:112

Psalm 119:145

Psalm 119:161

Psalm 125:4

Psalm 131:1

Psalm 138:1

Psalm 138:3

Psalm 139:23

Psalm 140:2

Psalm 141:4

Psalm 143:4

Psalm 147:3

Psalm 148:14

Proverbs 1:23

Proverbs 2:2

Proverbs 2:10

Proverbs 3:1

Proverbs 3:3

Proverbs 3:5

Proverbs 4:4

Proverbs 4:21

Proverbs 4:23

Proverbs 5:12

Proverbs 6:14

Proverbs 6:18

Proverbs 6:21

Proverbs 6:25

Proverbs 7:3

Proverbs 7:25

Proverbs 10:8

Proverbs 10:20

Proverbs 11:16

Proverbs 11:20

Proverbs 12:20

Proverbs 12:23

Proverbs 12:25

Proverbs 13:12

Proverbs 13:25

Proverbs 14:10

Proverbs 14:13

Proverbs 14:30

Proverbs 14:33

Proverbs 15:7

Proverbs 15:11

Proverbs 15:13

Proverbs 15:14

Proverbs 15:15

Proverbs 15:28

Proverbs 15:30

Proverbs 16:1

Proverbs 16:5

Proverbs 16:9

Proverbs 16:21

Proverbs 16:23

Proverbs 17:3

Proverbs 17:20

Proverbs 17:22

Proverbs 18:12

Proverbs 18:15

Proverbs 19:3

Proverbs 19:21

Proverbs 20:5

Proverbs 20:9

Proverbs 21:1

Proverbs 21:2

Proverbs 21:4

Proverbs 22:11

Proverbs 22:15

Proverbs 22:17

Proverbs 22:18

Proverbs 23:7

Proverbs 23:12

Proverbs 23:15

Proverbs 23:17

Proverbs 23:19

Proverbs 23:26

Proverbs 24:2

Proverbs 24:12

Proverbs 24:17

Proverbs 24:32

Proverbs 25:3

Proverbs 25:20

Proverbs 26:23

Proverbs 26:24
Proverbs 26:25
Proverbs 27:9
Proverbs 27:11
Proverbs 27:19
Proverbs 28:14
Ecclesiastes 2:1
Ecclesiastes 2:8
Ecclesiastes 2:10
Ecclesiastes 2:15
Ecclesiastes 2:20
Ecclesiastes 3:11
Ecclesiastes 3:17
Ecclesiastes 5:2
Ecclesiastes 5:20
Ecclesiastes 6:2
Ecclesiastes 7:2
Ecclesiastes 7:3
Ecclesiastes 7:4
Ecclesiastes 7:7
Ecclesiastes 7:22
Ecclesiastes 7:26
Ecclesiastes 8:5
Ecclesiastes 8:11
Ecclesiastes 9:3
Ecclesiastes 9:7
Ecclesiastes 10:2
Ecclesiastes 11:9
Ecclesiastes 11:10
Song of Solomon 3:1
Song of Solomon 3:2
Song of Solomon 3:3
Song of Solomon 3:4
Song of Solomon 3:11
Song of Solomon 4:9
Song of Solomon 5:2
Song of Solomon 5:4

Song of Solomon 5:6
Song of Solomon 8:6
Isaiah 1:5
Isaiah 6:10
Isaiah 7:2
Isaiah 7:4
Isaiah 9:9
Isaiah 10:12
Isaiah 13:7
Isaiah 14:13
Isaiah 15:4
Isaiah 15:5
Isaiah 16:11
Isaiah 19:1
Isaiah 19:3
Isaiah 19:10
Isaiah 19:19
Isaiah 21:4
Isaiah 26:8
Isaiah 29:2
Isaiah 29:13
Isaiah 30:14
Isaiah 30:29
Isaiah 35:4
Isaiah 38:3
Isaiah 40:11
Isaiah 42:25
Isaiah 44:20
Isaiah 46:8
Isaiah 46:12
Isaiah 49:21
Isaiah 51:7
Isaiah 57:1
Isaiah 57:11
Isaiah 57:15
Isaiah 59:13
Isaiah 60:5

Isaiah 61:1
Isaiah 63:4
Isaiah 63:17
Isaiah 65:14
Isaiah 66:14
Jeremiah 3:10
Jeremiah 3:15
Jeremiah 3:17
Jeremiah 4:4
Jeremiah 4:9
Jeremiah 4:14
Jeremiah 4:18
Jeremiah 4:19
Jeremiah 5:23
Jeremiah 7:24
Jeremiah 8:18
Jeremiah 9:8
Jeremiah 9:14
Jeremiah 9:26
Jeremiah 11:8
Jeremiah 11:20
Jeremiah 12:2
Jeremiah 13:10
Jeremiah 15:1
Jeremiah 15:16
Jeremiah 16:12
Jeremiah 17:1
Jeremiah 17:5
Jeremiah 17:9
Jeremiah 17:10
Jeremiah 18:12
Jeremiah 20:9
Jeremiah 20:12
Jeremiah 22:17
Jeremiah 23:9
Jeremiah 23:17
Jeremiah 23:20

Jeremiah 23:26
Jeremiah 24:7
Jeremiah 29:13
Jeremiah 30:24
Jeremiah 31:20
Jeremiah 31:33
Jeremiah 32:39
Jeremiah 32:41
Jeremiah 42:20
Jeremiah 48:29
Jeremiah 48:36
Jeremiah 48:41
Jeremiah 49:16
Jeremiah 49:22
Jeremiah 49:23
Jeremiah 51:46
Lamentations 1:20
Lamentations 1:22
Lamentations 2:11
Lamentations 2:18
Lamentations 2:19
Lamentations 3:13
Lamentations 3:41
Lamentations 3:65
Lamentations 4:3
Lamentations 5:15
Lamentations 5:17
Ezekiel 3:10
Ezekiel 6:9
Ezekiel 11:19
Ezekiel 11:21
Ezekiel 13:22
Ezekiel 14:3
Ezekiel 14:4
Ezekiel 14:5
Ezekiel 14:7
Ezekiel 18:31

Ezekiel 20:16
Ezekiel 21:6
Ezekiel 21:7
Ezekiel 21:15
Ezekiel 24:25
Ezekiel 25:6
Ezekiel 25:15
Ezekiel 27:25
Ezekiel 27:26
Ezekiel 27:27
Ezekiel 28:2
Ezekiel 28:5
Ezekiel 28:8
Ezekiel 28:17
Ezekiel 32:9
Ezekiel 33:31
Ezekiel 36:5
Ezekiel 36:26
Ezekiel 43:15
Ezekiel 43:16
Ezekiel 44:7
Ezekiel 44:9
Daniel 5:20
Daniel 7:4
Daniel 11:27
Daniel 11:28
Daniel 11:30
Hosea 5:4
Hosea 7:6
Hosea 7:14
Hosea 10:2
Hosea 11:8
Joel 2:12
Joel 2:13
Amos 7:10
Obadiah 1:3
Jonah 2:3

Nahum 2:10
Habakkuk 3:16
Zephaniah 3:14
Zechariah 7:10
Zechariah 7:12
Zechariah 10:7
Zechariah 12:5
Malachi 2:2
Malachi 4:6
Matthew 5:8
Matthew 5:28
Matthew 6:21
Matthew 9:2
Matthew 9:4
Matthew 9:22
Matthew 11:29
Matthew 12:34
Matthew 12:40
Matthew 13:15
Matthew 13:19
Matthew 15:8
Matthew 15:18
Matthew 15:19
Matthew 18:35
Matthew 19:8
Matthew 22:37
Mark 2:8
Mark 3:5
Mark 6:52
Mark 7:6
Mark 7:19
Mark 7:21
Mark 8:17
Mark 10:5
Mark 11:23
Mark 12:30
Mark 12:33

Luke 1:17	Acts 15:8	2 Corinthians 7:2
Luke 2:19	Acts 15:9	2 Corinthians 7:3
Luke 2:35	Acts 16:14	2 Corinthians 8:16
Luke 2:51	Acts 21:13	2 Corinthians 9:7
Luke 3:15	Acts 28:27	2 Corinthians 9:14
Luke 5:22	Romans 1:9	Galatians 4:6
Luke 6:45	Romans 1:21	Ephesians 1:18
Luke 7:13	Romans 1:24	Ephesians 3:17
Luke 8:12	Romans 1:31	Ephesians 4:18
Luke 8:15	Romans 2:5	Ephesians 5:19
Luke 10:27	Romans 2:15	Ephesians 6:5
Luke 12:29	Romans 2:29	Ephesians 6:6
Luke 12:34	Romans 5:5	Ephesians 6:7
Luke 16:15	Romans 6:17	Philippians 1:7
Luke 21:34	Romans 8:27	Philippians 4:7
Luke 24:25	Romans 9:2	Colossians 2:2
Luke 24:32	Romans 10:1	Colossians 3:1
John 5:42	Romans 10:6	Colossians 3:15
John 12:27	Romans 10:8	Colossians 3:16
John 12:40	Romans 10:9	Colossians 3:22
John 14:1	Romans 10:10	Colossians 3:23
John 14:27	Romans 15:6	Colossians 4:8
John 16:33	1 Corinthians 4:5	1 Thessalonians 2:4
Acts 1:24	1 Corinthians 10:6	1 Thessalonians 3:13
Acts 2:26	1 Corinthians 14:25	2 Thessalonians 2:17
Acts 2:37	2 Corinthians 1:9	2 Thessalonians 3:5
Acts 2:46	2 Corinthians 1:22	1 Timothy 1:5
Acts 4:32	2 Corinthians 2:4	1 Timothy 3:1
Acts 5:3	2 Corinthians 3:2	2 Timothy 2:22
Acts 7:39	2 Corinthians 3:3	Philemon 1:7
Acts 7:51	2 Corinthians 3:15	Philemon 1:12
Acts 8:21	2 Corinthians 4:1	Philemon 1:20
Acts 8:22	2 Corinthians 4:6	Hebrews 3:8
Acts 8:36	2 Corinthians 4:16	Hebrews 3:10
Acts 11:23	2 Corinthians 5:12	Hebrews 3:12
Acts 13:22	2 Corinthians 6:11	Hebrews 3:15
Acts 14:17	2 Corinthians 6:13	Hebrews 4:7

Hebrews 4:12
Hebrews 8:10
Hebrews 10:16
Hebrews 10:22
Hebrews 12:3
Hebrews 12:5
Hebrews 13:9
James 3:14
James 4:8
1 Peter 1:22
1 Peter 3:15
2 Peter 1:19
1 John 3:19
1 John 3:20
1 John 3:21
1 John 5:10
Revelation 1:3
Revelation 2:23
Revelation 17:17
Revelation 18:7

AFTERWORD

My son, Devin Upton, who will be four years of age at the time that this book is published, had an encounter with a child at a local health club that left me feeling angry and quite powerless. Unfortunately, I was not able to protect my child because I was at work when the incident took place. My wife gave me a phone call at work to inform me of what had happened. Apparently, a child that my son encountered that was no more than five years of age in the children's play area shoved Devin several times and informed him based upon his words that he did not like the color of his skin.

When a child as young as the one my son encountered begins to say things and exhibit such unacceptable behavior, then we as adults must pay close attention and strongly renew our efforts to teach our children to love other people regardless of their racial and cultural background. Most children tend to respond to others in their environment based upon the type of behavior that has been modeled in their home by their parents, older siblings, relatives and friends. We need to do everything that can possibly be done to reach any child that shows any signs of being afraid or intolerant of children that come from diverse racial and cultural backgrounds. If we fail to reach these children before it is too late then they will eventually become adults that will have nothing but hatred in their hearts for persons of color. We desperately need to begin to teach these children to love and appreciate people that come from different racial and cultural backgrounds. Otherwise, our nation will be destined to experience even more racial tension and conflict as it continues to become more racially diverse. Debra Van Ausdale and Joe R. Feagin, in their book entitled *The First R: How Children Learn Race and Racism* once again reminds us how adults play a major role in determining whether or not children will take on anti-racist behavior or racist behavior.

In the book, Ausdale and Feagin say,

> Obviously, the realities of race and racism do not start with children.... We adults are a primary source. And they are champions at showing exactly how masterful human beings can be in perpetuating racial-ethnic hatred, discrimination, and inequalities. Attempts to change their behavior, however, may be ineffective until we adults change our own. Watching children at work with racism is like watching ourselves in a mirror. They will not unlearn and undo racism until we do.[29]

ENDNOTES

1. *Churches Need to Promote Diversity Researcher Says* Matt Vandebunte. Grand Rapids Press 17 Nov. 2001, MI.
2. Environmental Racism: Refers to any environmental policy, practice, or directive that differentially affects or disadvantages (whether intended or unattended) individuals, groups, or communities based on race or color. (Dr. Robert D. Bullard, Professor of Sociology and Director of the Environmental Justice Resource Center at Clark Atlanta University).
3. Department of the Treasury and The Department of Justice, National Church Arson Taskforce, Fourth Year Report for the President, (Washington, D.C.: Department of the Treasury and the Department of Justice, 2000) 4.
4. Ibid., 4.
5. *A Cause for Mourning.* Lynne Duke, Washington Post 4 April 2000, Washington, D.C.
6. *Coca-Cola Settles Race Suit.* CNNMONEY. 16 Nov. 2000, http://www.moneycnn.com/2000/11/16/companies/coke/
7. Lott Apologizes Again For Terrible Remark. Thomas B. Edsall and Dan Balz, Washington Post December 2002, Washington, D.C.
8. U.S. Census Bureau, Dynamic Diversity: Projected Changes in U.S. Race and Ethnic Composition 1995 to 2050, (Washington, D.C.: U.S. Census Bureau, 2000) 8.
9. Ibid., 8.
10. Ibid., 1,11.
11. Ibid., 8.
12. Ibid., 8.
13. U.S. Census Bureau, Profiles of General Demographic: 2000. (Washington, D.C.: U.S. Census Bureau) 1.
14. *Demographics Figures Tell the Story of a Changing America.* Jonathan Tilove, Newhouse News Service, Grand Rapids Press 15 Jul. 1998, MI.
15. Jonathan Earle, The Routledge Atlas of African American History. (New York, New York:Routledge, 2000) 22.
16. Ibid., 22.

17. U.S. Census Bureau, Population Projections of the United States by Age, Sex, Race and Hispanic Origin: 1995 to 2050, Current Population Reports, P25-1130, (Washington, D.C.: U.S. Census Bureau, 1996) 1, 11 - 13.

18. Ibid., 1, 17.

19. Ibid., 1.

20. Ibid., 1.

21. Ibid., 13.

22. Ibid., 1 - 2.

23. U.S. Census Bureau, Profiles of General Demographic: 2000. (Washington, D.C.: U.S. Census Bureau) 1.

24. U.S. Bureau of the Census, Population Projections of the United States by Age, Sex, Race and Hispanic Origin: 1995 to 2050, Current Population Reports, P25-1130, (Washington, D.C.: U.S. Census Bureau, 1996) 13.

25. President's Initiative on Race, The Advisory Board Report to the President, One America in the 21st Century (Washington, D.C.: President's Initiative on Race, 1999) 23.

26. Ibid., 23.

27. *Prejudice Ranks as Top Problem in Future.* Will Lester, The Associated Press, Grand Rapids Press 10 Oct. 1999, MI.

28. Ibid., 1 - 4.

29. Debra Van Ausdale and Joe R. Feagin, The First R (Lanham, Maryland: Rowman & Littlefield, 2001).

SPECIAL PERMISSIONS
GRANTED TO REPRINT QUOTES

FINAL QUESTIONS

Please take a few moments and respond to the following questions:

- How has God used this book to impact your life? _____

  _____

  _____

  _____

  _____

- Have you uncovered any prejudice, bigotry or racism in your heart?

  _____

  _____

  _____

  _____

  _____

- Did you repent of any sin after reading this book? _____

  _____

  _____

  _____

  _____

- What did you learn about bigotry, prejudice, and racism that you did not know before? _____

  _____

  _____

  _____

  _____

- What action steps(s) do you plan to take to address bigotry, prejudice, and racism? _____

  _____

  _____

  _____

  _____

  _____

The author is interested in receiving written comments from you regarding the above questions or any information regarding how this book has positively impacted your life. You may forward any written correspondence to:

Mailing Address
Upton Consulting
P.O. Box 1351
Grand Rapids, MI 49501
e-mail: rsuptongr@aol.com

Photograph by Rachel R. Rydbeck

Photograph by Rachel R. Rydbeck

ABOUT THE AUTHOR

Robert Upton is a Senior Consultant with Upton Consulting, an organizational management consulting firm that provides a wide range of services to corporate and non-profit organizations. Upton Consulting is based in Grand Rapids, Michigan, and is managed and staffed by partners: Robert Upton and Sandra Upton, both of whom have a combined fifteen years of experience in assisting organizations in improving how they function—and more importantly, how they manage and lead their people resources.

Robert is a gifted public speaker, special event organizer, community leader, and evangelist. He has devoted a great deal of his life to addressing the issues of race and inequality. Robert and his wife Sandra and their two children Alexis & Devin reside in Grand Rapids, Michigan. They presently attend Grand Rapids First Assembly of God Church in Grand Rapids, Michigan.

To speak with the author or obtain further information, please call:
(616) 243-5129

or simply write to:

Upton Consulting
P.O. Box 1351
Grand Rapids, MI 49501-1351
e-mail: rsuptongr@aol.com